When Christ Shall Come

When Christ Shall Come

VITAL DISCERNMENT FOR END TIMES,
PRETERISM, AND OUR BLESSED HOPE

Don Green

When Christ Shall Come:
Vital Discernment for End Times, Preterism, and Our Blessed Hope

Don Green

Copyright © 2024 Donald Green

ISBN: 978-0-9987156-3-6

Cover design and typeset by www.greatwriting.org

Printed in the United States of America

Trust the Word Press
575 Chamber Drive
Milford, OH 45150

TRUST THE WORD
PRESS
BIBLICAL THINKING FOR BIBLICAL LIVING

Contents

To Chris Hamilton, a most treasured and trusted brother in Christ, who personifies the highest virtues of biblical integrity, wisdom, and leadership.

❖

Introduction

I did not set out to write a book on eschatology ("the study of last things").

But when word got out that I had written an academic paper on the doctrine of preterism, enough people expressed interest that I thought I should put it in print to help the body of Christ.

About that same time, war broke out in Israel in October 2023. The congregation at Truth Community Church started asking questions about the future of Israel and dispensationalism that intersected with my work on preterism. At that point, it seemed good to me to expand the scope of the book to give an overview of the biblical teaching on end times and its implications for faith and obedience today. Christians need to see that the return of Christ has a vital bearing on our approach to the Christian life.

To those who are familiar with the many theological controversies surrounding eschatology, it will quickly become apparent that I have not attempted to address all that could be said. I have pastoral objectives in the first three chapters, driven by my acquaintance with young believers who have no perspective on the return of Christ at all. That material is geared toward a general audience.

The material on preterism is academic in nature, originally written for the requirements of my Master of Theology degree in the spring of 2000. Time constraints at this point in my life do not allow me to update the work by interacting with anything published since that time. I realize that limitation falls short of an academic ideal, but the biblical principles and historical facts that refute preterism are timeless.

The problem with preterism is that it never comes alone. In my observations, some of its proponents present a different view of Christian liberty, sanctification, and the purpose of the church than I believe is biblical. Exposing the fallacy of preterism will do much to protect those under my pastoral care from those other dangers. That's why I need to put the academic material in the last half of this book into print.

The title of this book comes from the final verse of the hymn "How Great Thou Art." It expresses the blessed hope and humble worship that should animate the heart of all true believers as they contemplate the return of Christ. My prayer is that the Lord would increase those affections in all who take and read the pages that follow:

> When Christ shall come with shout of acclamation
> And take me home, what joy shall fill my heart!
> Then I shall bow in humble adoration
> And there proclaim, my God how great Thou art.
>
> Then sings my soul, my Savior God, to Thee:
> How great Thou art, how great Thou art!
> Then sings my soul, my Savior God, to Thee:
> How great Thou art, how great Thou art!

Jim Holmes has applied his excellent design and editorial skills to my manuscript. Dr. Peter Sammons gave me timely counsel pertaining to eschatology and the 1689 London Baptist Confession of Faith. My patient wife, Nancy, has reviewed all that follows and made several important suggestions to improve what you now have before you. I'm grateful for all their support.

May God use this book greatly to His glory.

Don Green
December 2023
Cincinnati, Ohio

1

What Happens Next?

As He was sitting on the Mount of Olives, the disciples came to Him privately, saying, "Tell us, when will these things happen, and what will be the sign of Your coming, and of the end of the age?"
(Matthew 24:3)

This chapter is a lightly edited transcript of my sermon at Truth Community Church from May 3, 2020.

Bible students eventually must confront the question of what happens next in the unfolding of God's plan for human history. Too much Scripture is prophetic in nature to do otherwise.

We must guard ourselves against flippant, easy answers—and those who propose them. The biblical material on future events is massive. One writer says that 27% of the Bible involves predictive material—some 8,352 verses out of the total of 31,124 verses in the Bible.[1] In one manner or another, over 8,300 of our current English verses were looking to something in the future at the time that they were written.

Why would I start with that statistic? It should give us all pause. The sheer volume of material should caution us against undue dogmatism when we speak about what will happen in the future. S. Lewis Johnson, a longtime seminary professor and pastor, said in a sermon:

> It is necessary for us to have a great deal of humility when we seek to interpret the many details of the prophetic word. . . . We are studying a very difficult subject . . . in which we are trying to put together a number of passages from the Word of God. It is amazing how much of the Bible is still concerned with prophecy. Trying to put it together into one coherent whole is a very difficult task.[2]

1 J. Barton Payne, *Encyclopedia of Biblical Prophecy*, (New York: Harper & Row, 1973), 681.

2 S. Lewis Johnson, "Premil Calendar, Future Events," 6; transcript avail-

Charles Spurgeon spoke with similar restraint:

> I am no prophet nor the son of a prophet, neither do I profess to be able to explain all the prophecies of this blessed Book. I believe that many of them will only be explained as the events occur which they foretell.[3]

It should be apparent that eschatology is a difficult subject. The volume of biblical material cautions us. Superior Bible teachers with decades of experience caution us. The mere fact that, for now, we are only spending one chapter on this topic shows that I am only trying to give a satellite overview without delving into debates that have filled books for decades.

An Overview of End Times

So what has God revealed to us about what will happen in the future? Let's start with an overview statement:

> Jesus Christ will one day return to earth to bring human history to a close. He will judge the living and the dead. After that, He will usher in an eternal state in which God will bless the saints and they will glorify Him forever. The wicked will be cast into everlasting torment away from the presence of the Lord and from the glory of His power.

That brief overview gives us the foundation upon which to build the rest of this chapter.

One day, Jesus Christ will return to earth. The world will be permanently altered by His return. His coming will also bring a time of judgment upon all humanity. Those who are in Christ will be received into heaven. Those who are not in Christ will

able at sljinstitute.net (accessed 11/24/23).

3 Charles Spurgeon, *Exploring the Heart and Mind of the Prince of Preachers*, ed. Kerry James Allen (Oswego, IL: Fox River Press, 2005), 144.

be judged for their sins and cast into a place of eternal torment as the just punishment for all of their sins. Those events will fix the eternal destinies of men as God establishes a new heaven and a new earth (cf. Rev 21:1).

Those are the key things to understand. If you get lost in the details of other aspects of future events, the relative simplicity of those doctrines will be a compass to re-orient you to the things that matter the most. If you grasp those truths, you have a basic understanding of what happens next in God's plan for human history.

Admittedly, that summary oversimplifies things. Within that broad framework, theologians see important aspects much differently. I acknowledge that. But I am not trying to settle any disputes about the rapture, the tribulation, the millennium, future judgment, or the eternal state right now. I am only establishing a framework so those other doctrines can be seen in their proper light.

A Perspective on Differing Views

As I have read on eschatology over the years, I have come to the opinion that it is difficult to find an unbiased presentation of different eschatological systems. Advocates of all views—be they premillennial, amillennial, or postmillennial—often are not forthcoming about the weaknesses of their own positions. Social media posts in particular are notorious for misrepresenting what others teach and hiding the weaknesses of their own position. They create the impression that eschatology is an easily resolved matter if others were not theologically dense and obtuse.

That's not true. Every system of interpretation of future prophecy faces difficult questions. We cannot avoid the fact that the study of biblical end times is complex.

Beyond that, I also pause over the fact that teachers with whom I otherwise agree on biblical authority, the nature of God, the person and work of Christ, and the sovereignty of God in salvation often disagree with each other on eschatological matters. That does not mean we should not strive for our own convictions about eschatology. It does not mean the matter of biblical end times is not important. If that were the case, I wouldn't be writing this book. But those differences should teach us to be measured in our words (cf. Proverbs 29:20).

I may disagree with an amillennialist like Anthony Hoekema or a postmillennialist like Loraine Boettner. But those men were not fools who treated Scripture lightly. It would violate Christian love and integrity to denigrate such men over eschatology. At the same time, my amillennialist and postmillennialist brothers would do well to acknowledge that John MacArthur, for example, is not a rube simply because he sees eschatology differently than they do.

By all means, we should teach our convictions as I will do below. But in light of the complexity of the material and that better men than us differ on these things, we should watch our tongues even if we find it necessary to warn against the consequences of opposing views. Many of the men with whom I disagree on end times still hold my respect and would be welcome to teach from my pulpit on other matters.

With that foundation laid, I am happy to be forthcoming regarding my own views. I am not amillennial. I do not believe that the present age in which we live is the millennium. I do not believe that Satan is presently bound. I do not believe that the church has replaced the nation of Israel. I believe that those who try to limit the debate about the millennium to a single text in Revelation 20 are guilty of a false reduction of the issues. I reject the interpretive decisions that lead to all those conclusions.

Likewise, I am not postmillennial in its various manifestations. I do not believe that the world will grow increasingly righteous through the preaching of the gospel or the imposition of biblical law on society. I believe both Scripture and thousands of years of human experience point us decisively away from that position.

That's the negative side.

On the positive side, I believe that the Abrahamic, Davidic, and New Covenants have implications for the still future history of national Israel. I believe that the New Testament extends the teaching of the Old Testament prophets rather than reinterpreting them. While holding those views, I also distance myself decisively from many who call themselves dispensationalists (for reasons explained in Appendix B).

Thus, while I am not trying to give the final word on anything in this book, I'm also not speaking blindly without awareness of other viewpoints.

With all of those qualifications in place, let's consider what Scripture seems to be teaching about what comes next in God's program. I will lay out six aspects in broad sequence with some basic biblical texts that undergird that understanding.

What happens next? In sequence, I believe (1) the rapture; (2) the tribulation; (3) the Second Coming; (4) the millennium; (5) final judgment; and (6) the eternal state. Those six segments of future events will follow the present age in God's plan. I will consider them, ever so briefly, in what follows.

The Rapture

The rapture refers to that time when Jesus Christ will come from heaven for His people. The dead in Christ and the Christians who are alive at that time will be raised to meet Him in the air.

> But we do not want you to be uninformed, brethren, about those who are asleep, so that you will not grieve as do the rest who have no hope. For if we believe that Jesus died and rose again, even so God will bring with Him those who have fallen asleep in Jesus. For this we say to you by the word of the Lord, that we who are alive and remain until the coming of the Lord, will not precede those who have fallen asleep. For the Lord Himself will descend from heaven with a shout, with the voice of the archangel and with the trumpet of God, and the dead in Christ will rise first. Then we who are alive and remain

will be caught up together with them in the clouds to meet the Lord in the air, and so we shall always be with the Lord. (1 Thess. 4:13-17)

I believe this passage teaches that Christ comes and calls forth those Christians who had previously died and also those who are alive at the time. He calls both the dead and living in Christ and brings them to Himself and into heaven. The rapture is "imminent," meaning that it could happen at any time (which is different than saying it necessarily will happen soon).

The rapture event will include a time in which the people of Christ will appear before Him at the judgment seat of Christ.

> Therefore, being always of good courage, and knowing that while we are at home in the body we are absent from the Lord—for we walk by faith, not by sight—we are of good courage, I say, and prefer rather to be absent from the body and to be at home with the Lord. Therefore we also have as our ambition, whether at home or absent, to be pleasing to Him. For we must all appear before the judgment seat of Christ, so that each one may be recompensed for his deeds in the body, according to what he has done, whether good or bad. (2 Cor. 5:6-10)

Paul is speaking here of believers appearing before Christ at the judgment seat of Christ. This is not a judgment to determine the eternal destiny of Christians, as if it were an open question whether believers would go to heaven or hell. That's not the point of this judgment. Christ has already atoned for all of our sins by shedding His blood at the cross. That secures our eternal home in heaven.

Rather, the judgment seat of Christ is a time in which He evaluates our Christian lives to reward us for following Him. Christ will look at the totality of our obedience, evaluate it, and reward us for our faithfulness to Him. Somehow, He will apportion blessing according to His grace and wisdom based on the way we responded to the life, resources, and opportunities He gave to us.

The judgment seat of Christ, then, invests our lives with eternal significance. Somehow, in a way I don't profess to grasp fully, the way we live as Christians will affect the blessing we receive in glory. That motivates us to godly living. Beyond that, we trust Christ to do what is right with it all.

In summary, Christ will rapture His people, gather them to Himself, and carry out a reward-focused judgment that He gives to His people at that time.

The Tribulation

After the rapture comes a time known as the tribulation period. Once Jesus Christ has removed His people from the world, a time of trouble will come upon the remaining inhabitants of the earth.

The tribulation is a time when God pours out judgment on the unbelieving world. Much of the world's population will perish under the wrath of God. Their physical lives will end as God pours out His judgment on their rebellion.

> Then I heard a loud voice from the temple, saying to the seven angels, "Go and pour out on the earth the seven bowls of the wrath of God." So the first angel went and poured out his bowl on the earth; and it became a loathsome and malignant sore on the people who had the mark of the beast and who worshiped his image. The second angel poured out his bowl into the sea, and it became blood like that of a dead man; and every living thing in the sea died. Then the third angel poured out his bowl into the rivers and the springs of waters; and they became blood. And I heard the angel of the waters saying, "Righteous are You, who are and who were, O Holy One, because You judged these things; for they poured out the blood of saints and prophets, and You have given them blood to drink. They deserve it." And I heard the

altar saying, "Yes, O Lord God, the Almighty, true and righteous are Your judgments." (Rev. 16:1-7)

There is much more on this in Scripture. It is not my purpose to explore it all. The Bible teaches us to expect a future time when God judges the earth through His holy angels. He will righteously and justly bring consequences upon the unsaved for their rejection of Christ and their persecution of God's people. It will be a terrifying time.

The future judgment of God enables us to persevere through times of unjust treatment. We can trust God to settle all accounts. The wickedness of the world will not go unpunished. These are lofty themes that give us perspective on the human events that tend to preoccupy our minds.

The Second Coming

After the tribulation, Christ will return to earth to establish His kingdom.

> Immediately after the tribulation of those days the sun will be darkened, and the moon will not give its light, and the stars will fall from the sky, and the powers of the heavens will be shaken. And then the sign of the Son of Man will appear in the sky, and then all the tribes of the earth will mourn, and they will see the Son of Man coming on the clouds of the sky with power and great glory. And He will send forth His angels with a great trumpet and they will gather together His elect from the four winds, from one end of the sky to the other. (Matt. 24:29-31)

We get another picture of the Second Coming:

> And I saw heaven opened, and behold, a white horse, and He who sat on it is called Faithful and True, and in righteousness He judges and wages war. His eyes are a flame of fire, and on His head are many diadems; and He

has a name written on Him which no one knows except Himself. He is clothed with a robe dipped in blood, and His name is called The Word of God. And the armies which are in heaven, clothed in fine linen, white and clean, were following Him on white horses. From His mouth comes a sharp sword, so that with it He may strike down the nations, and He will rule them with a rod of iron; and He treads the wine press of the fierce wrath of God, the Almighty. And on His robe and on His thigh He has a name written, "King of kings, and Lord of lords." (Rev. 19:11-16)

As we read on in Revelation, we find that Christ will bind Satan so that he is no longer able to deceive the nations.

Then I saw an angel coming down from heaven, holding the key of the abyss and a great chain in his hand. And he laid hold of the dragon, the serpent of old, who is the devil and Satan, and bound him for a thousand years; and he threw him into the abyss, and shut it and sealed it over him, so that he would not deceive the nations any longer, until the thousand years were completed; after these things he must be released for a short time. (Rev. 20:1-3)

In summary, Christ comes visibly to earth after a time of tribulation with glory and in power. He pours out wrath upon the unbelieving world and also binds Satan so that the devil is no longer able to work his deceptive powers upon the nations.

The Millennium

As you continue in Revelation, you read of a 1000-year age in which Jesus Christ reigns on earth, which is known as the millennium.

> Then I saw thrones, and they sat on them, and judgment was given to them. And I saw the souls of those who had been beheaded because of their testimony of Jesus and because of the word of God, and those who had not worshiped the beast or his image, and had not received the mark on their forehead and on their hand; and they came to life and reigned with Christ for a thousand years. The rest of the dead did not come to life until the thousand years were completed. This is the first resurrection. Blessed and holy is the one who has a part in the first resurrection; over these the second death has no power, but they will be priests of God and of Christ and will reign with Him for a thousand years. (Rev. 20:4-6)

Notice how "a thousand years" is repeatedly emphasized *after* Christ comes to earth. His followers are now with Him. Where is Christ? He's on earth. What are the saints doing with Him? They are reigning with Christ, on earth, for 1000 years.

What is the point of the millennium? Throughout the Old Testament, God promised the nation of Israel through His prophets that there would be a future time of blessing for them. Even though God sent them into exile to discipline them for their sin and rebellion, He promised that He would remember the promises that He would raise up a descendent of David to reign on the earth from Jerusalem (cf. 2 Sam. 7).

After the time of David, the Old Testament prophets repeatedly spoke in glowing terms about a future kingdom for Israel. God promised His people that He would establish this kingdom because He loved them and would maintain loyal love to them.

Those promises mean that the integrity and truthfulness of

God is at stake. Will He keep His promise, or no? With those things in mind, we read the following:

> "Say to them, 'Thus says the Lord GOD, "Behold, I will take the sons of Israel from among the nations where they have gone, and I will gather them from every side and bring them into their own land; and I will make them one nation in the land, on the mountains of Israel; and one king will be king for all of them; and they will no longer be two nations and no longer be divided into two kingdoms. They will no longer defile themselves with their idols, or with their detestable things, or with any of their transgressions; but I will deliver them from all their dwelling places in which they have sinned, and will cleanse them. And they will be My people, and I will be their God. My servant David will be king over them, and they will all have one shepherd; and they will walk in My ordinances and keep My statutes and observe them. They will live on the land that I gave to Jacob My servant, in which your fathers lived; and they will live on it, they, and their sons and their sons' sons, forever; and David My servant will be their prince forever. I will make a covenant of peace with them; it will be an everlasting covenant with them. And I will place them and multiply them, and will set My sanctuary in their midst forever. My dwelling place also will be with them; and I will be their God, and they will be My people. And the nations will know that I am the LORD who sanctifies Israel, when My sanctuary is in their midst forever."'" (Ezek. 37:21-28)

God will establish a kingdom for the nation Israel over which a descendant of David will sit as King. This King will reign over the earth and the people will serve Him in righteousness and keep His commandments.

Well, friends, nothing like that has happened since God made this promise through Ezekiel roughly 600 years before the time of Christ. The nations have not gathered. The nations have not seen the glory of the Lord. Another prophet says:

> The earth will be filled with the knowledge of the glory of the LORD, as the waters cover the sea. (Hab. 2:14)

My friend, look at the world around you. Can we say that anything has remotely approached such a universal knowledge of God and His glory? The millennium will be the still-future fulfillment of that promise. The whole world will see that God did in fact keep His promise to His people in that coming reign of righteousness and peace. That is the purpose of the millennium.

Final Judgment

The millennium is not quite the end of this earth. God will exercise a final judgment on unbelievers.

> When the thousand years are completed, Satan will be released from his prison, and will come out to deceive the nations which are in the four corners of the earth, Gog and Magog, to gather them together for the war; the number of them is like the sand of the seashore. And they came up on the broad plain of the earth and surrounded the camp of the saints and the beloved city, and fire came down from heaven and devoured them. And the devil who deceived them was thrown into the lake of fire and brimstone, where the beast and the false prophet are also; and they will be tormented day and night forever and ever. (Rev. 20:7-10)

Satan is briefly released to manifest that he is still the wicked fallen angel that he had always been. Not even 1000 years of confinement changed his nature. And further, man is still subject to the devil's deception after all that time. At long last, God puts an end to it all.

> Then I saw a great white throne and Him who sat upon it, from whose presence earth and heaven fled away, and no place was found for them. And I saw the dead, the great and the small, standing before the throne, and books were opened; and another book was opened, which is the book of life; and the dead were judged from the things which were written in the books, according to their deeds. And the sea gave up the dead which were in it, and death and Hades gave up the dead which were in them; and they were judged, every one of them according to their deeds. (Rev. 20:11-13)

God has raised unbelievers bodily from the dead for their final judgment.

> Then death and Hades were thrown into the lake of fire. This is the second death, the lake of fire. And if anyone's name was not found written in the book of life, he was thrown into the lake of fire. (Rev. 20:14-15)

This final judgment gives a sober accent to all of life on earth today. The Bible says that unbelievers have a final appointment with God. In this terrifying event, God will look on men and women in their unforgiven sin and judge them. He will send them away into the lake of fire with the devil, the beast, the false prophet, and all unbelievers of all time forever. Their destiny is publicly declared and eternally sealed. There will be no escape.

The awful nature of eternal judgment should inform the way we study and speak of end time events. It is tragic that many want to speculate on details which Scripture has not made known. What ultimately matters is that sinners are on a fast track to damnation if they do not repent and believe in the Lord Jesus Christ.

When we look at the reality of future events, we're brought back to the reason Jesus Christ came in His *first* coming. He came to give His life as a ransom for sinners (cf. Matt. 20:28).

He suffered on the cross as a substitute sacrifice as God poured His wrath on Christ instead of those who would believe in Him. On the third day, Christ was raised from the dead, having accomplished redemption from sin for those who humbly come to Him for forgiveness.

The nature of final judgment means that every unbeliever must face this question: what will happen to you on that day, when you are alone before God and the opportunity for salvation has passed you by? The age of grace will be closed. The door will be slammed shut. All that is left is to face the fury of a righteous God against all of your ungodliness and unrighteousness.

Oh, my friend. Is that what you want? Is that the destiny that you would choose for yourself? Consider the state of your sinful soul and cry out in humble repentance for Christ to save you. He will. In love He promises to snatch you from this horrible fate that is awaiting unbelieving men. Others may disbelieve, that does not need to hinder you. Jesus said:

> I am the way, and the truth, and the life; no one comes to the Father but through Me. (John 14:6)

When the final judgment is rendered, what happens then?

The Eternal State

The eternal state will be the final removal of the curse of sin. Christians will enjoy unhindered fellowship with the God of our salvation. We will crown Christ with many crowns, the Lamb upon His throne, and we will be with Him in a beautiful, perfect city of worship.

> Then I saw a new heaven and a new earth; for the first heaven and the first earth passed away, and there is no longer any sea. And I saw the holy city, new Jerusalem, coming down out of heaven from God, made ready as a bride adorned for her husband. And I heard a loud voice

from the throne, saying, "Behold, the tabernacle of God is among men, and He will dwell among them, and they shall be His people, and God Himself will be among them, and He will wipe away every tear from their eyes; and there will no longer be any death; there will no longer be any mourning, or crying, or pain; the first things have passed away." (Rev. 21:1-4)

God will banish all sin and sorrow as He brings us into this place of perfection—the holy city, the new Jerusalem. We will know peace, joy, and such profound satisfaction in His goodness that all notions of regret will be forever taken away. He will bestow on us full and perfect bliss as we see our Savior face to face, forever and ever without end. The picture is expanded in what follows.

He showed me a river of the water of life, clear as crystal, coming from the throne of God and of the Lamb, in the middle of its street. On either side of the river was the tree of life, bearing twelve kinds of fruit, yielding its fruit every month; and the leaves of the tree were for the healing of the nations. There will no longer be any curse; and the throne of God and of the Lamb will be in it, and His bond-servants will serve Him; they will see His face, and His name will be on their foreheads. And there will no longer be any night; and they will not have need of the light of a lamp nor the light of the sun, because the Lord God will illumine them; and they will reign forever and ever. (Rev. 22:1-5)

Nothing in our present lives begins to compare to the joy we will have when God fulfills this promise. My Christian friend, we will gaze on the face of the One who loved us and gave Himself up for us (cf. Gal. 2:20). The faith which was weak on earth will become sight. We will see Him, not as through a mirror, but in all His glorious fullness. We will be in the presence of the One who suffered for our souls.

One wonderful aspect of the eternal state is that we will be fully and finally *home*. The environment will not seem alien to us, but will be the most natural and joyful place we could ever be. The glory will overwhelm us and cause us to burst forth in praise. Unhindered by sin and the limitations of our flesh, we will give the highest worship, praise, and gratitude to Christ.

That final outcome is what we live for as believers. Nothing in this world compares to the great glory of that eternal reality that will be ours in Christ.

So now what? How do all these things about future events affect the way we live now? Scripture brings us back to the present and tells us:

> Everyone who has this hope fixed on Him purifies himself, just as He is pure. (1 John 3:3)

Would you take biblical end times seriously, my Christian friend? Scripture does not lead you to speculate about obscure points of prophecy. Christ calls you to take your holiness and sanctification seriously. He calls you to be patient in adversity because eternal blessing is coming. He calls you to trust Him and live in peace, content to be under His sovereign and loving hand.

In light of what the future holds, we live in holiness today. When Christ comes, we want to be found living for Him. We live in peace. We pursue righteousness. And we look for His return. The next to last verse of the Bible is a word from Christ and a response from His people:

> He who testifies to these things says, "Yes, I am coming quickly." (Rev. 22:20)

That's what happens next. And what is our heart response?

> Amen. Come, Lord Jesus. (Rev. 22:20)

Come, Lord Jesus. Having seen everything that Scripture says about end times, we submit with that simple prayer. We yield to His sovereign purpose and wait for the final deliverance that He has promised to us.

For those who long for His appearing, Scripture gives a final word of benediction. It is my prayer for you, dear reader, as we close.

The grace of the Lord Jesus be with all. Amen. (Rev. 22:21)

2

Be on the Alert

Be on the alert then, for you do not know
the day nor the hour.
(Matthew 25:13)

This chapter is a lightly edited transcript of my sermon at Truth Community Church from August 15, 2021.

The way the world is now is not the way that it will always be. We are looking forward to a supernatural intervention of the Lord Jesus Christ in world history in which He will bring all things to judgment and accomplish the eternal purpose which the Father set into motion at creation in Genesis 1:1.

Our Lord will return visibly to establish His kingdom on earth. Even the church ordinance of communion proclaims the Lord's death *until He comes* (cf. 1 Cor. 11:26). True Christians live with a great sense of wonder and anticipation as they look to the return of Christ.

This future return of the Lord Jesus Christ is central to biblical Christianity. Mockers may say, as Peter mentions in one of his letters, "Where is the promise of His coming?" (2 Peter 3:4). But God has shown us in His Word that this world is transient. The ultimate goal of history will be accomplished at the return of Christ.

In the meantime, we have a window of life between now and Christ's return. We must ask how these future things affect our view of life. How does biblical thinking about the return of Christ affect biblical living today? God intends for us to make those connections in our worldview.

Frankly, some biblical teaching over the past century has not helped us apply the reality of Christ's return to the way we live. Over the years, I've had deep concern over a lot of prophetic teaching that has been popular in the church. Teachers and laymen alike occupy themselves by trying to name the date—or at least, general time frame—on which Christ is supposedly going to return.

That is a serious mistake. Jesus made plain, as we shall see, that no one knows the date or time of His return. So the pattern that looks at world events, and tries to make direct connections to the day Christ returns, is seriously misguided. It is a threat to the well-being of your soul when they leave out the application of how the return of Christ affects the way you should live today. Scripture is clear that, as we ponder the return of Christ, we are to live with wisdom and holiness in the meantime. That's the way that we are to think. That's the way we are to live.

God forbid that there would be anyone reading these pages that takes a casual or merely academic interest in future events without serious consideration of what it means for his personal life and holiness. We must ask God to deliver us from that unbiblical mindset that speculates on future events while living ungodly lives. It's completely unthinkable.

Scripture repeatedly warns against that spiritual cancer.

> The day of the Lord will come like a thief, in which the heavens will pass away with a roar and the elements will be destroyed with intense heat, and the earth and its works will be burned up. Since all these things are to be destroyed in this way, what sort of people ought you to be in holy conduct and godliness, looking for and hastening the coming of the day of God, because of which the heavens will be destroyed by burning, and the elements will melt with intense heat! But according to His promise we are looking for new heavens and a new earth, in which righteousness dwells. Therefore, beloved, since you look for these things, be diligent to be found by Him in peace, spotless and blameless. (2 Peter 3:10-14)

The Bible says there is a specific way for you to live in response to the future coming of Christ. You are to live in holiness. You are to be found in peace, spotless and blameless, pursuing sanctification, if you know the Lord Jesus Christ and you confess these things to be true.

In other words, the soon return of Christ has a profound impact on the way that we establish our priorities. Let me ask you sympathetically, my friend: do you even think about these things? Have you considered the consequences?

Since the earth is going to be destroyed and Christ is going to return, we hold this life loosely, realizing that it's all temporary. The environment and our very lives are transient and passing away. That has great consequences for how we set our affections and how we use our time and resources.

Jesus taught a parable to impress the importance of this upon us in Matthew 25. This passage comes in the midst of Matthew 24-25, a text known as the Olivet Discourse. Jesus is teaching His disciples about future things to come and used this parable to help them understand how they should respond to the reality of His future return:

> Then the kingdom of heaven will be comparable to ten virgins, who took their lamps and went out to meet the bridegroom. Five of them were foolish, and five were prudent. For when the foolish took their lamps, they took no oil with them, but the prudent took oil in flasks along with their lamps. Now while the bridegroom was delaying, they all got drowsy and began to sleep. But at midnight there was a shout, "Behold, the bridegroom! Come out to meet him." Then all those virgins rose and trimmed their lamps. The foolish said to the prudent, "Give us some of your oil, for our lamps are going out." But the prudent answered, "No, there will not be enough for us and you too; go instead to the dealers and buy some for yourselves." And while they were going away to make the purchase, the bridegroom came, and those who were ready went in with him to the wedding feast; and the door was shut. Later the other virgins also came, saying, "Lord, lord, open up for us." But he answered, "Truly I say to you, I do not know you." Be on

the alert then, for you do not know the day nor the hour. (Matt. 25:1-13)

When Jesus taught in parables, He was making one primary point. We're not supposed to look for great meaning in every single detail of a parable, but find the main point and take it to heart. In this passage, the main point of our Lord is to develop wisdom in His disciples, so that they will live rightly in light of His future return.

This parable tells us that a wise man or woman will have spiritual urgency to respond. It is critical to prepare *now* for what will surely happen in the *future*. You must respond to the gospel of Jesus Christ and bring forth the fruit of repentance to prepare yourself for that coming day.

But if you foolishly give yourself over to the things of this world with no regard for the things of Christ, something bad is going to happen. Christ will return at a time when you don't expect it. And then—it will be too late. Your soul will be eternally lost and condemned.

My friend, if you are not ready for the time when Christ returns—or when you meet Him in death—the eternal loss will be unspeakable. You will be left outside His kingdom to face eternal judgment with no second opportunity to come to Him. You will be sent away without an invitation to return. Consequently, pay heed and look after the well-being of your eternal soul while there is time.

If you're unfamiliar with the cultural background of this parable, it may sound unusual upon first reading it. The customs of that day are not the customs of ours. Some basic historical context will help us understand what Jesus is saying.

The Background to the Parable
•••

The disciples of Christ had earlier asked Him about the sign of His coming. They were interested in future events.

> As He was sitting on the Mount of Olives, the disciples came to Him privately, saying, "Tell us, when will these things happen, and what will be the sign of Your coming, and of the end of the age?" (Matt. 24:3)

Everything Jesus says in Matthew 24-25 is framed by the questions His disciples asked. In what follows, Jesus answers their questions. He explains aspects of His Second Coming and what they should do about it. As we read on, we see the repeated emphasis in His response.

> Just as the lightning comes from the east and flashes even to the west, so will the coming of the Son of Man be. (Matt. 24:27)

> Then the sign of the Son of Man will appear in the sky, and then all the tribes of the earth will mourn, and they will see the Son of Man coming on the clouds of the sky with power and great glory. (Matt. 24:30)

> Therefore be on the alert, for you do not know which day your Lord is coming (Matt. 24:42)

> For this reason you also must be ready; for the Son of Man is coming at an hour when you do not think He will. (Matt. 24:44)

Jesus answers the disciples by emphasizing the sudden and unexpected nature of His return. It is of highest urgency, of utmost, critical priority, to be prepared for it *in advance.*

It is precisely here that those of you who are not in Christ are vulnerable. The coming of Christ will be unexpected. It will be sudden. At that time, Christ will separate believers unto His presence as unbelievers enter a time of judgment. Stated differently, Christ will separate humanity based on their relationship (or lack thereof) to Him.

Friend, you simply must face that reality and calculate it in your heart. In some ways, the most critical truth for you to know is that we all have a time appointed to appear before Christ and give an account to Him. Scripture makes this abundantly clear.

> It is appointed for men to die once and after this comes judgment. (Heb. 9:27)

Whether you die and face Christ in judgment, or whether you're alive at the time of His return and face Him in judgment, you must take into account that certain appointment.

I'm reminded of the preacher that once said, "I preach as a dying man to dying men." We're all passing away. We should not presume upon having another opportunity to hear truth and being able to respond to it.

You should treat this as your last opportunity to consider these things. It's that urgent. The coming of Christ and His judgment will be cataclysmic. In light of that, what should you know and what should you do? What does this parable in Matthew 25:1-13 teach you?

Christ Is Certainly Coming

In Matthew 25:1-13, Jesus is referring to what would have been a familiar marriage custom among the Jews. Jewish marriages, at that time, were arranged by the family and couples had little say in whom they would marry. Weddings were big events that involved the entire community.

After the couple had been chosen for each other, there was a formal period of about 12 months that led up to the actual wedding called the betrothal period. This was more binding to the couple and the families than our modern engagement periods.

Many things happened in that twelve-month interlude. For one, the groom would prepare the home in which he and his bride would one day live. During that same time, the bride would prepare her wedding clothes and make other preparations for the gallant affair. The bride's family would plan the wedding feast and the wedding day festivities. The delay and activity during the preceding year meant that much anticipation developed for the special time to come.

When the wedding itself came, it was an elaborate affair. The bride and groom were like a queen and a king in their attire and presence. The projection of royalty emphasized the importance of the moment and the sacred nature of the institution of marriage. In other words, the entire culture came together to mark the profound moment as a couple embarked on a new life together (cf. Gen. 2:24-25).

Weddings, simply stated, were a *really* big deal and *everyone* knew in advance when a wedding was on its way.

After the wedding itself, there would be a procession for the couple, something like a parade, through the village at the end of the day. The bridegroom and bride separated briefly to make preparations for the evening.

The groom would then take his attendants to the bride's house (i.e., the house at which she had lived with her parents). There he would meet her and they would proceed to their new home. The entire village celebrated during the procession as the groom took his bride from her former house to the new home where they would start their new life together.

Crucially for our purposes, the procession normally took place toward the end of the day as darkness was descending. So as the bride and groom were making their way from her old house to their new house, the people of the village lined the way, standing with torches to light the way. Everyone wanted to participate. Everyone *could* participate. Those with lit lamps could share in the festivities at the new home. The only caveat was that each person was responsible to bring his own torch (or, "lamp" as it is translated here).

In light of that background, what would any prudent person

do? Who would not do whatever is necessary to join in the joy of the celebration? It's simple. You make sure, in advance, that you are ready when the procession begins.

You make sure your lamp is ready with the necessary oil to fuel it so that you can participate in the way that's expected of you. If your lamp was not prepared, you would miss it all. You would be excluded. You would be on the outside looking in.

It was not uncommon for the bride and groom to be delayed in making the procession. The village never knew precisely what time they would arrive. They knew that they *would* come, but sometimes the time was delayed. Crucially, you had to be ready for *whenever* it was, even if it was later than you had anticipated.

All of that helps us understand Jesus' teaching in Matthew 25:1-13. Jesus focuses on the preparation of the young ladies who knew about the wedding and the subsequent procession.

> The kingdom of heaven will be comparable to ten virgins. (Matt. 25:1)

Jesus compares the anticipation of His return to earth with the expectation of a wedding procession. He compares something familiar to His first audience to draw out a principle that will apply to spiritual matters that are unfamiliar.

> Five of them were foolish, and five were prudent. For when the foolish took their lamps, they took no oil with them. But the prudent took oil in flasks along with their lamps. (Matt. 25:2-4)

The word for "foolish" is the Greek word from which we get our term "moron." The five virgins who did not prepare for the procession were unthinkably senseless and irresponsible. They were behaving with inexcusable neglect in light of a certain event that was coming.

By contrast, the prudent virgins displayed practical wisdom and common sense to the expected events of the day. They knew a procession was coming and that it was important to be a part of it. Since participation required a burning lamp, they had to have oil. They made sure to make provision before the time arrived. In that way, they were certain to be ready when the time came.

Jesus' hearers would have sympathized with the common sense of the prudent virgins and, in like manner, would have been shocked at the behavior of the foolish virgins. With full knowledge of the risk, they refused to prepare for the coming event. The bridegroom was certainly coming. The only question was when.

In like manner, my friend, Jesus Christ is certainly coming again to earth. The only question is when. We don't know when He will appear, but we know that He undoubtedly will. You will stand before Christ and what will happen to you then? Will you enter the kingdom or be left behind?

As Jesus develops the parable, He injects an element of delay.

> Now while the bridegroom was delaying, they all got drowsy and began to sleep. (Matt. 25:5)

There's no moral culpability in the fact that they got drowsy. The night was getting long and their eyes were getting heavy. The problem is not that they failed to fight off understandable sleep. The issue was the preparation that was, or was not, made beforehand.

Jesus uses the bridegroom's return to picture His own return to earth. Christ is coming again. He will return. The uncertainty of delay does not change the fundamental reality. Our Lord spoke in a similar way elsewhere in Scripture:

> Do not let your heart be troubled; believe in God, believe also in Me. In My Father's house are many dwelling places; if it were not so, I would have told you; for I go to prepare a place for you. If I go and prepare a place for you, I will come again and receive you to Myself, that

where I am, there you may be also (John 14:1-3).

In keeping with those words, Jesus did go away to heaven in His ascension (see Acts 1:9-11). But His absence is temporary. He will return in the same way that He left. He will come back for His own. Christians—and only Christians—will have a place with Him when He does.

Scripture is clear that Christ will certainly come again. Each one of us must answer what that means for us today. That brings us to the next point of this parable.

Prepare for the Certain Return of Christ

Since Christ is certainly coming, my friend, you should certainly use your life and time to prepare for His return. We see that point clearly as we continue in the parable. In the middle of their drowsy sleep, a shout shatters their slumber. The time has come.

> But at midnight there was a shout, "Behold, the bridegroom! Come out to meet him." (Matt. 25:6)

The time for preparation is over. The bridegroom is present. They must go out immediately for the procession. The ten virgins no longer control their fate. Events are happening on the bridegroom's timetable. His actions determine everything else. They can only respond based on their prior preparation.

> Then all those virgins rose and trimmed their lamps. The foolish said to the prudent, "Give us some of your oil, for our lamps are going out." But the prudent answered, "No, there will not be enough for us and you too; go instead to the dealers and buy some for yourselves." (Matt. 25:7-9)

We must avoid misplaced sympathy for the foolish virgins. They had been given time to prepare. But they carelessly and foolishly did not act upon what they knew. The moment had come. The opportunity for preparation had passed them by. They were not ready.

The prudent virgins lit their lamps and went out to meet the triumphant bridegroom. As a result, those wise young ladies were part of the celebration. They shared in the joy of the occasion with the bridegroom. There was no reason for them, in the custom of the day, to share their oil. Why should they risk their own lamps going out when the foolish virgins had failed to prepare themselves?

That lack of preparation was morally culpable. Through negligence or rebellion, they had refused to act. The fact that they failed to do what was necessary brought vast consequences which the prudent virgins were not responsible to correct. Each one stood on her own.

The foolish virgins rushed out, desperately hoping against hope to get some oil in time to join. But it's too late.

> While they were going away to make the purchase, the bridegroom came, and those who were ready went in with him to the wedding feast; and the door was shut. (Matt. 25:10)

The foolish virgins went out, after hours as it were, hoping that the 7-Eleven would have what they needed. But there was nothing. The bridegroom had come and gone. Those who were prepared were welcomed, joined the procession, and entered into the festivities.

But then the door is shut. The feast begins. What a blessing to share in the bridegroom's joy! But for anyone else, the opportunity is over. Nevertheless, the foolish virgins try to crash the party.

> Later the other virgins also came, saying, 'Lord, lord, open up for us.' (Matt. 25:11).

"Let us in! We're here now. We're ready now." But they only hear a devastating rejection.

But he answered, "Truly I say to you, I do not know you."
(Matt. 25:12)

It was too late. They had squandered the opportunity that
they knew was coming, and it is now their immeasurable loss.
The door is closed. Admission is refused. The foolish virgins
are left to bear the consequences of their own foolishness.
They were missing the feast that they could have attended if
only they had taken the simple preparation that others did,
and common sense required.

There is no excuse. Their rejection is devastating, final, and
complete.

Those hearing the story in the first century when Jesus
taught it would have affirmed the outcome because they would
have understood the custom. The foolish virgins are not sympathetic figures. They are objects of accountability and judgment. The entire parable tells them, "There is no excuse for
what you have done. You will bear dire consequences as a
result." They deserved to be excluded because they did not
care enough to take it all seriously.

The parable is now over. It is only left for Jesus to draw out
the moral implications for those disciples who had asked Him
about future events. He makes the point that He would have
all to learn.

Be on the alert then, for you do not know the day nor the
hour. (Matt. 25:13)

Jesus indicates the primary lesson we are to draw from His
parable. What shall we do in response to His certain return? It
is breathtakingly simple.

You must be ready. You must be on the alert. You must prepare for the return of Christ. My friend, in light of His future
coming, you have a non-delegable responsibility to prepare
your soul to meet Him. He may return unexpectedly. You may
meet Him in death. You may meet Him in the skies.

The circumstances of that future occasion do not matter in

comparison to the more transcendent issue: will you be wise? Will you get ready? *Are* you ready? Do you know Christ? Have you ever sensed responsibility to prepare your soul for that great coming event?

It *will* happen. The only question is when.

Jesus Christ calls us to be ready. What does that look like? If you don't know Christ, your preeminent responsibility is to repent of your sin and to turn to Him by faith to save you and bring you into His kingdom so that you will be safe in His hands when He does return. Nothing else matters in comparison. If you're not ready when Christ comes, it will be devastating—no matter what kind of life you've lived on earth.

> For what will it profit a man if he gains the whole world and forfeits his soul? Or what will a man give in exchange for his soul? For the Son of Man is going to come in the glory of His Father with His angels, and will then repay every man according to his deeds. (Matt. 16:26-27)

> But God said to him, "You fool! This very night your soul is required of you; and now who will own what you have prepared?" So is the man who stores up treasure for himself, and is not rich toward God. (Luke 12:20-21)

Jesus gave a similar warning earlier in the gospel of Matthew. He pictures two kinds of people standing before Him on Judgment Day.

> Not everyone who says to Me, "Lord, Lord," will enter the kingdom of heaven, but he who does the will of My Father who is in heaven will enter. Many will say to Me on that day, "Lord, Lord, did we not prophesy in Your name, and in Your name cast out demons, and in Your name perform many miracles?" And then I will declare to them, "I never knew you, depart from Me, you who practice lawlessness." (Matt. 7:21-23)

"I never knew you." That anticipates the words of the bridegroom in Matthew 25:12 to the foolish virgins: "I do not know you." Many will be crushed on that day. It cries out for all to exercise wisdom today.

> Therefore everyone who hears these words of Mine and acts on them, may be compared to a wise man who built his house on the rock. And the rain fell, and the floods came, and the winds blew and slammed against that house; and yet it did not fall, for it had been founded on the rock. (Matt. 7:24-25)

The prudent virgins and the wise builder alike prepared beforehand for the coming of Christ and the storm of judgment. Their soul was ready to meet their Maker and Judge. But many will not act with wisdom.

> Everyone who hears these words of Mine and does not act on them, will be like a foolish man who built his house on the sand. The rain fell, and the floods came, and the winds blew and slammed against that house; and it fell and great was its fall. (Matt. 7:26-27)

The whole building came down on them. The ruin was complete, final, and irreversible. It's a picture of those sent away to eternal judgment because they had not secured their souls in Christ during their lives, while they had opportunity to do so.

That is a devastating picture of what lies ahead for all who neglect Christ in this life. It will be no excuse that you were too busy. That merely insults Christ by saying that there are other things more important to you than Him. All those with that attitude—to say nothing of those that mock and despise Him—face a miserable outcome and eternal fate.

Suddenly the rumble will occur and the building will collapse.

Suddenly the bridegroom will shout and there will be no time to enter the feast.

Oh, my dear friend. What will happen to you then?

Metaphorically speaking, your shoulders will droop and your head will hang low. But that's not the end. You will turn to walk away, but you will find an angel waiting to usher you into a place that you do not want to go—a place of judgment.

Not only will you be excluded from the kingdom, you will be taken somewhere against your wishes. Judgment has come. You ignored Christ in this life; now He rejects you for the next. He sends you into eternal judgment where hell is real, painful, and eternal.

Oh, oh, the horror of being unprepared! Won't you look afresh at the familiar promise, offered freely and in love, to save you from such a wretched fate?

> For God so loved the world, that He gave His only begotten Son, that whoever believes in Him shall not perish, but have eternal life. (John 3:16)

My friend, you're here and you have time. Christ freely invites you to come to Him for salvation now. He will certainly receive you if you will truly turn to Him.

In other words, this is your moment to prepare for the inevitable reality to come. God is graciously giving you another opportunity—will it be the last?—to come to Christ now for salvation. There's still time for you. But you must not delay. Unless you repent, you will perish (cf. Luke 13:1-5).

By glorious contrast to you who truly know Christ by faith: take heart. The bridegroom knows who carries the lamp of faith. He will gladly welcome you into His eternal kingdom at His coming.

Christ remembers His own and no one can pluck you out of His hand (cf. John 10:28-30). Christ will never turn away one who is truly His.

Have you ever just missed a really bad car wreck? You slam on the brakes just in time and think, "Oh, my. That would have been horrific." But you realize, "Oh, I'm safe. Thank God."

In light of Matthew 25:1-13, those of us in Christ can thank

Him that He delivered us from so great a peril as a Christless death and eternity. We thank God for His grace that came to us and brought the gospel to us. We thank Him for the Holy Spirit, who worked in our hearts and brought Christ to us. We thank Him that our future is safe by the shed blood of the Lord Jesus Christ. We look to the future and realize that we have security in Christ. We respond with a great sense of gratitude, relief, and a life of heartfelt obedience.

My Christian friend, what a blessing to know now that you'll be welcome then. Now that you're ready, the Bridegroom can come at any time as far as you're concerned.

Praise God from whom all blessings flow.

3

On That Great Day

Beloved, now we are children of God, and it has not appeared as yet what we will be. We know that when He appears, we will be like Him, because we will see Him just as He is.
(1 John 3:2)

This chapter is a lightly edited transcript of my sermon at Truth Community Church from May 24, 2020.

I try to avoid the concept of having a "favorite" Bible verse. All of God's Word is inspired by the Holy Spirit and precious. I don't think we should elevate one text over another.

But I also realize that the Lord applies some passages to our hearts in special ways. Over the years, 1 John 3:1-3 has been one of those texts in my life. It is a source of great aspiration to every believer in Christ.

> See how great a love the Father has bestowed on us, that we would be called children of God; and such we are. For this reason the world does not know us, because it did not know Him. Beloved, now we are children of God, and it has not appeared as yet what we will be. We know that when He appears, we will be like Him, because we will see Him just as He is. And everyone who has this hope fixed on Him purifies himself, just as He is pure. (1 John 3:1-3)

Christians are greatly blessed. Our sins are forgiven in Christ. God rules over all things by His providence. Our heavenly Father knows our needs and has numbered the hairs on our heads. Our lives may be uncertain from our perspective, but God guides all things so that they work together for our good. There are no contingencies or surprises with God.

As a result, we rest in His sovereign goodness toward us. He cares for us (cf. 1 Peter 5:8). Goodness and lovingkindness will surely follow us all the days of our lives and we will dwell in the house of the LORD forever (cf. Ps. 23:6). Those are great blessings.

Yet Scripture points us to more.

The Bible tells of a future event for believers in Christ that will dwarf everything else by comparison. What happens on that great day is the subject of our text in 1 John 3.

The Context of the New Birth

By way of context, the apostle John had just said that God gives birth to His children in the act of regeneration.

> If you know that He is righteous, you know that everyone also who practices righteousness is born of Him.
> (1 John 2:29)

The Holy Spirit uses the Word of God to impart new life to someone who had previously been dead in sin. He sets us free from the stranglehold of sin and Satan and brings us into the kingdom of God's beloved Son (cf. Col. 1:13-14).

Those enormous truths remind us that Christianity is a supernatural, spiritual "religion." We do not follow rules of mere human morality. The ethics of Christianity are derivative of the supernatural act of God in saving His people.

When God gives the new birth—that is to say, when He makes someone a new creation in Christ (cf. 2 Cor. 5:17)—He changes his life. Christianity is not self-reformation based on human effort and wisdom. The power of God is at work.

That's why, in 1 John 2:29, John can say that righteous living is one mark of being a true Christian. If you know that (1) God is righteous; and (2) God gives birth to His children through the act of regeneration; then it's obvious that (3) the true children of God will somehow reflect the righteousness of their Father. After all, human children bear the characteristics of their biological parents. In a far greater way, true Christians bear the spiritual characteristics of the One who gave birth to them.

God is holy. God is loving. Somehow, those aspects of His character express themselves in the lives of everyone who has truly been born again—no matter how imperfectly. The child of God displays the character of God because he shares in the nature of God. That is the flow of thought as we enter into 1 John 3.

Don't let the chapter break mislead you. The chapter and verse divisions in our Bibles were introduced long after the Scriptures were originally written. They help us locate the text and break it down into manageable portions as we read. I'm grateful to God for His providence in making that happen. But those chapter breaks are only markers—they do not in themselves represent a change in the flow of thought from the biblical author.

Here in 1 John 3:1, the apostle is not introducing a new, unrelated thought to what he had just said in 2:29. He is building on it. He expands on the majestic reality of the new birth with our position in Christ, our hope in Christ, and our response to Christ.

Our Great Position in Christ

John reflects on the fact of our new birth. To be born of God is to be a child of God. God has brought us into His family. That is an act of staggering love to unworthy sinners (cf. Romans 5:8).

> See how great a love the Father has bestowed on us, that we would be called children of God; and such we are. (1 John 3:1)

John is saying, "Stop and consider what I just said. Reflect on the fact that we are children of God." It is a wonderful reality and John calls attention to it forcibly. He is astonished at the privilege.

My friend, if you think about your life, it should astonish you as well to be a Christian.

There you were, born in sin, hostile in mind, and a rebel against God (cf. Eph. 2:1-3). You were blind, ignorant of spiritual things, and your heart was hard and cold. Left to your own devices, you would have gone deeper and deeper into the nature of that existence.

And yet here you are, my Christian friend—alive in Christ. Your sins have been forgiven. The Spirit of God has planted a new nature within you and dwells within you. God is working to conform you to the likeness of Jesus Christ. Then, when your life on earth is done, you will enter heaven, leaving behind this world of sin and sorrow to enter a realm of blessedness in the presence of Christ, which is very much better.

> Do not let your heart be troubled; believe in God, believe also in Me. In My Father's house are many dwelling places; if it were not so, I would have told you; for I go to prepare a place for you. If I go and prepare a place for you, I will come again and receive you to Myself, that where I am, there you may be also. (John 14:1-3)

It is astonishing that we have received such grace. We will live forever in a place Christ has prepared for us instead of receiving the punishment our sins deserve. Who could have imagined such blessings upon unworthy men and women like us?

To be a true Christian is the noblest position anyone in the world could have. It is better to have Christ in poverty than to be the President of the United States without Him. Our position in Christ is infinitely more significant than anything that is happening to us today. We have received a great inheritance from our heavenly Father that no one can take away. We are secure in Christ and no one can pluck us from His hand (cf. John 10:28-30).

That great position in Christ is what John is calling attention to. God has given us favor that we do not deserve. He has been patient with our many sins. He has done for us things we could not do for ourselves. His love, patience, grace, and kindness are just overwhelming.

We are in the family of God.

As a result, all the frustrations, sorrows, and anxieties of life—finances, relationships, physical weaknesses—yield to a greater reality. To be united with Christ should elicit a sense of wonderment from your heart as you contemplate your great position in Him.

I venture to say that almost all the travails of our souls can be traced to the fact that we've lost sight of that. We see only the problems rather than the surpassing gift that God has given to us in Christ. To be a child of God is to have far more than anything the world could give. If there were 10,000 worlds and they all belonged to you, they would not be worthy to be compared to being in Christ.

That has consequences. Our union with Christ affects the way we relate to the world. Unsaved people may be hostile to us over our love for Christ and His kingdom. John addresses that as he continues:

> For this reason the world does not know us, because it did not know Him. (1 John 3:1)

That verse helps us understand our present experience. In the past, the world was hostile to Christ and crucified Him. In the present, the world rejects Him. We who are disciples of Christ will get the spillover effect of that hatred and rejection. They will reject us because of our identification with Christ. It is inevitable.

We should expect varying degrees of difficulty as we live in a fallen world that is hostile to God. We carry the spiritual image of Christ with us, and to the world our presence is an aroma of death (cf. 2 Cor. 2:14-16). Our presence reminds them of God's holiness and their sinfulness. That is unpleasant to them, so it is not surprising they react against us. John picks up this point later:

Do not be surprised, brethren, if the world hates you. We know that we have passed out of death into life, because we love the brethren. He who does not love abides in death. (1 John 3:13-14)

The very nature of our identity in Christ means we will find opposition from the world. That should not discourage us. It is an inherent part of the cost and privilege of following Christ. Indeed, it is a blessing in disguise.

Blessed are those who have been persecuted for the sake of righteousness, for theirs is the kingdom of heaven. Blessed are you when people insult you and persecute you, and falsely say all kinds of evil against you because of Me. Rejoice and be glad, for your reward in heaven is great; for in the same way they persecuted the prophets who were before you. (Matt. 5:10-12)

When we suffer for Christ at the hands of an unfriendly world, we should understand why it is happening. The world did not know Christ and did not welcome Him. It is to be expected that it will not know and welcome us. In another place, Jesus said:

If the world hates you, you know that it has hated Me before it hated you. If you were of the world, the world would love its own; but because you are not of the world, but I chose you out of the world, because of this the world hates you. Remember the word that I said to you, "A slave is not greater than his master." If they persecuted Me, they will also persecute you; if they kept My word, they will keep yours also. (John 15:18-20)

Take heart, my Christian friend. It is easy to respond in anger, defensiveness, or simmering resentment, isn't it? But Scripture says it is actually a gift from God to suffer for the sake of Christ.

> For to you it has been granted for Christ's sake, not only to believe in Him, but also to suffer for His sake. (Phil. 1:29)

If Christ has ordained that you experience rejection for His sake, your spiritual duty is to accept it as coming from Him and be glad that you can identify with Him in His sufferings (cf. Phil. 3:10-11). Whatever the secondary human causes may be, God orders our circumstances to conform us to the image of His dear Son. We can accept that, knowing that God will work everything together for good for those who love God and are called according to His purpose (cf. Rom. 8:28). He uses even what evil people intend against us for our ultimate good (cf. Gen. 50:20).

In the midst of persecution, we are comforted by the goodness of God that brought us into His family. Nothing can separate us from the love of God which is in Christ Jesus our Lord (cf. Rom. 8:38-39). Rather than being downcast, we rejoice over a greater reality that transcends it all. Our heavenly Father loves us. He has chosen us out of the world. He will bless us in the end.

We live in confidence. We live in joy because one day we will be in heaven where we will be rejoicing even more.

These enduring truths shape the way Christians should live. Our great position in Christ changes the way that we live, think about life, and how we understand everything that happens to us along the way. Our Elder Brother in heaven represents us at the right hand of the Father. That is where life and satisfaction are found.

That leads us to our second point from this passage.

Our Great Hope
························

After developing our joy as children of God walking in a hostile world, John takes the thought even further.

> Beloved, now we are children of God . . . (1 John 3:2)

He returns to the primary thought driving this entire text. We are born of God. We are children of God who belong to the family of God. The wonderful truth tumbles rapidly through his pen and onto the page. He goes on and says:

> . . . and it has not appeared as yet what we will be.
> (1 John 3:2)

Yes, we are children of God. But we have not yet entered into the full significance of it all. We do not yet have full possession of it all. We are children, but greater blessing from God awaits us.

Stop right there.

It would be enough simply to be a child of God and walk through life in that blessed position. That alone would be far more than we deserve. That alone would be enough to fill our hearts with overflowing joy.

But John says that's not the half of it. Yes, you are a child of God. Yet, that present position in Christ is only a down payment on still *greater* things to come. A greater glory will one day dwarf our present dignity.

> Now we are children of God, and it has not appeared as yet what we will be. (1 John 3:2)

John confesses his own ignorance *as an apostle* of the fullness of what is to come. Even as he writes under the inspiration of the Holy Spirit, he doesn't fully grasp it all (cf. 1 Peter 1:10-12). A great day is coming where the children of God will be changed. We don't know the details but we know something for certain.

We know that when He appears, we will be like Him, because we will see Him just as He is. (1 John 3:2)

The simplicity of his language—he uses words a child could say—almost obscures the infinite magnitude of his meaning. We simply must take the time to let it all sink in.

Whenever Christ appears, something will happen to us. It is staggering. It is stunning. I don't have the vocabulary to do it justice. What we find here is *exponentially* greater than anything that this world could ever offer to us. It is *exponentially* greater than anything that we will experience in this life.

John is telling us our personal eschatological destiny. The ultimate goal—the final purpose—for which God saved you has nothing to do with anything that will happen in the course of your lifetime.

No, the ultimate purpose is right here. One day, Jesus Christ will appear. He will manifest Himself visibly to all His children. Somehow, He will call us to Himself, and when He does that—whenever He does that—He will supernaturally transform us into His very likeness as we see Him in the fullness of His glory.

We will be made like Him because we will see Him just as He is.

I don't know what all that entails. How could I, when John himself did not know? But I know enough from Scripture to say this: It will be surpassingly great. It will be infinitely glorious. It will be far more abundantly beyond all that we ask or think in this life (cf. Eph. 3:20-21).

These staggering words from John take us into a completely different realm.

Jesus Christ is going to appear in great glory. When He comes, we who belong to Him will see Him as He really is, in resurrected glory. And more than that—when we see Him, we will be forever changed. He will change us into a new condition. We will be transformed by His glory into the likeness of His glorious image. We will share in His perfect holiness. We will somehow share in His resurrected glory and perfection.

The sin, and the despair, and the frailty, and the guilt of this life will instantly be forgotten as we enter into the realm that Christ has lovingly been storing up for us for the past 2,000 years. It will be great. *Really* great. Great far beyond all else, I say!

Scripture speaks elsewhere of our coming transformation.

> For our citizenship is in heaven, from which also we eagerly wait for a Savior, the Lord Jesus Christ; who will transform the body of our humble state into conformity with the body of His glory, by the exertion of the power that He has even to subject all things to Himself. (Phil. 3:20-21)

One necessary point of clarification. We will not be *equal* to Christ. We will *never* be equal to Christ. We could never be equal to Christ because we will never be uncreated God. We are creatures who had a beginning. We will never be equal to the Creator who had no beginning. We will give worship to Him but never receive worship for ourselves.

With that stated, what lies ahead for us is a realm of glory of conformity to the image of Christ, in which we belong to Him and in which we belong to be where He is.

> We will see Him just as He is (1 John 3:2).

Now, we worship by faith. We pray by faith. But on that great day, faith will become sight. We will behold the infinite grandeur of the glory of Jesus Christ face-to-face. We will be there with Him as a child of God, belonging to Him, after He has opened the fullness of His kingdom to us.

The realm of that glory will be so magnificent that we have to be changed in order to absorb the resplendent majesty of it all. Christ will fit us for His heavenly kingdom in a way that will endure forever and ever without end.

That place of blessedness will be a place of supreme, immeasurable, infinite joy, infinite glory, infinite wonder, and infinite love that is utterly without sin, utterly without sorrow, utterly without tears, utterly without evil people to diminish or threaten it, utterly without any human authority to take it away from us, and all of that will utterly belong to us, as we behold the glory of the Lord Jesus Christ face to face.

> As for me, I know that my Redeemer lives, and at the last He will take His stand on the earth. Even after my skin is destroyed, yet from my flesh I shall see God; whom I myself shall behold, and whom my eyes will see and not another. My heart faints within me! (Job 19:25-27)

> When Christ, who is our life, is revealed, then you also will be revealed with Him in glory. (Col. 3:4)

> There will no longer be any curse; and the throne of God and of the Lamb will be in it, and His bond-servants will serve Him; they will see His face, and His name will be on their foreheads. (Rev. 22:3-4)

My Christian friend, this is your certain future. This is what God has prepared for you before the foundation of the world. It is unspeakably great. Martyn Lloyd-Jones expressed it this way:

> Do you know you are destined [to] see Him as He is? Blessed, glorious vision to see the Son of God in all His glory, as He is, face-to-face—you standing and looking at Him and enjoying Him for all eternity. It is only then that we will begin to understand what He did for us, the price He paid, the cost of our salvation. Oh, let us hold onto this! Shame on us for ever grumbling or complaining; shame on us for ever saying that the lot of the Christian is hard; shame on us for ever objecting to the demands of this glorious gospel; shame on us for ever half-heartedly worshiping, praising and loving His honor and His glory. You and I are destined for that vision glorious; we shall see Him as He is, face-to-face.[4]

4 Martyn Lloyd-Jones, *Life in Christ* (Wheaton: Crossway, 2002), 291-292.

Somehow, that is the glory into which every Christian will enter. We will be in the presence of the eternal Son of God and we will personally see the glory of His bodily resurrection. You will see Him more clearly than you now see the pages of this book. That is the ultimate and final reality that awaits us. That is our great *hope*.

I ask you: in light of our great position and our great hope, doesn't that utterly transform the way you look at the passing issues of today? How could it not? Doesn't that make today's troubles seem much smaller by comparison? How could it not?

So what exactly do you *do* with these wonderful truths today?

Our Glad Response

The future return of Christ is meant to influence the way that you live. It changes your preoccupation with earthly things to a love for the far greater realities that await you.

This passing life has nothing to offer you by comparison. Our great hope in Christ elevates our existence into something glorious, even if nothing changes in our outward circumstances. There are implications for life in light of the reality of being a child of God.

> And everyone who has this hope fixed on Him purifies himself, just as He is pure. (1 John 3:3)

Our future hope produces purity today. *Everyone* who has this hope pursues a life of biblical sanctification (to use the theological term). There are no exceptions. You cannot continue in sin if you are in the family of God and that great hope is really in your heart.

In our modern usage, "hope" has come to refer to a kind of a wish that may or may not happen. Someone may hope his favorite team wins the championship, but in light of their lack of talent, they probably won't.

That is not the sense of New Testament hope at all. In Scripture, hope is a confident expectation that is grounded in the sure promise of an omnipotent God. We look forward to that which we do not yet have, but which we most certainly one day will.

As we consider our great hope, think for a moment about the One who gave it to us. The God who saved us, the God who caused us to be born again, is a God of all power. He has the ability to perform His will without hindrance from man. He is a God of truth and He has promised all that lies ahead for all of His children.

An omnipotent and faithful God has promised this great transformation to His children. We first respond to Him with a confident expectation that He will truly bring this to pass. We respond with faith, in other words (cf. Heb. 11:6).

But we go further. We also remember that the God who has promised this to us is also a holy God. We trust Him, yes, but we also fear Him enough to turn from sin and pursue righteousness (cf. Prov. 3:7). As we dwell on His good promise for the future, we renew our pursuit of practical, biblical righteousness today.

There is an inevitable turn to holy living if we truly believe we will see Christ face to face. The apostle repeatedly says in 1 John that obedience to God is the mark of true faith.

> If we say that we have fellowship with Him and yet walk in the darkness, we lie and do not practice the truth. (1:6)

> By this we know that we have come to know Him, if we keep His commandments. The one who says, "I have come to know Him," and does not keep His commandments, is a liar, and the truth is not in him. (2:3-4)

> If you know that He is righteous, you know that everyone also who practices righteousness is born of Him. (2:29)

> Little children, make sure no one deceives you; the one who practices righteousness is righteous, just as He is righteous. (3:7)

> By this the children of God and the children of the devil

are obvious: anyone who does not practice righteousness is not of God, nor the one who does not love his brother. (3:10)

This is the love of God, that we keep His commandments; and His commandments are not burdensome. (5:3)

We know that no one who is born of God sins; but He who was born of God keeps him, and the evil one does not touch him. (5:18)

As you can see, the matter of holy living is a repeated theme in John's epistle. *That* is the context for this statement:

Everyone who has this hope fixed on Him purifies himself, just as He is pure. (1 John 3:3)

Obedience is the mark of every true Christian. An unrepentant life of indifference to God and hostility toward His commandments is the mark of someone who has never been born again, no matter what they may say with their lips.

Consequently, if we are truly born again, and if we have truly fixed our hope on seeing Christ in the future, we will look at our current relationships and responsibilities and seek to apply ourselves to live out righteousness in the lives God has given us. Beyond that, we will seek to know the God of our salvation by reading His Word, seeking Him in prayer, and having fellowship with His people (cf. Acts 2:42; Heb. 10:24-25).

Our great hope of seeing Christ leads to a great response. We turn from the present world to lead a life that is devoted to the glory of the God of our salvation (cf. 1 Cor. 10:31). We seek first His kingdom and His righteousness (cf. Matt. 5:6, 6:33).

My Christian friend, if you really have this hope in your heart, your responsibility is to pursue the righteousness that is revealed in Christ and His Word.

If you read this and realize that you are not a Christian,

know that this great hope is freely offered to you. The time has come for you to repent and to leave the world behind. Come to Christ who lovingly offers you forgiveness of all of your sins based on His atoning death at the cross of Calvary and promises you, even you, all the riches of which I have spoken. They can be yours. Christ is fully willing to give them to you. He simply calls you to come in humble repentant faith and receive Him as your Lord, as your Master, as your Savior, and He will make you a child of God as well.

> Truly, truly, I say to you, he who hears My word, and believes Him who sent Me, has eternal life, and does not come into judgment, but has passed out of death into life. (John 5:24)

> For this is the will of My Father, that everyone who beholds the Son and believes in Him will have eternal life, and I Myself will raise him up on the last day. (John 6:40)

> These have been written so that you may believe that Jesus is the Christ, the Son of God; and that believing you may have life in His name. (John 20:31)

My prayer is that you will indeed come.

4

An Explanation of Preterism

Be diligent to present yourself approved to God as
a workman who does not need to be ashamed,
accurately handling the word of truth.
(2 Timothy 2:15)

In the first chapter, I referred to a time of future tribulation that will come upon all the earth. Not all professing Christians hold to that doctrine. These men, called preterists, believe in one form or another that time of judgment has already occurred. It is to that teaching we now turn.

Some Key Terms

The word "preterist" comes from the Latin term *praeteritus*, which means "gone by," or past.[5] Among other things, preterists believe that Jesus' predictions in Matthew 24-25 (the "Olivet Discourse") were fulfilled in A. D. 70 during the destruction of Jerusalem. Their position is grounded in their interpretation of certain "time references" in Matthew 10:23,[6] 16:28,[7] and 24:34,[8] which they believe demand that Jesus' prophecies be fulfilled within the lifetime of His hearers.[9] Preterists also

5 Kenneth Gentry, "The Great Tribulation Is Past," in *The Great Tribulation: Past or Future?*, (Grand Rapids: Kregel, 1999), 13.

6 "But whenever they persecute you in one city, flee to the next; for truly I say to you, you shall not finish going through the cities of Israel until the Son of Man comes."

7 "Truly I say to you, there are some of those who are standing here who will not taste death until they see the Son of Man coming in His kingdom."

8 "Truly I say to you, this generation will not pass away until all these things take place."

9 R. C. Sproul, *The Last Days According to Jesus*, (Grand Rapids: Baker, 1998), 24-25.

maintain that the book of Revelation was written before A. D. 70 and finds its fulfillment in the destruction of Jerusalem.[10]

At this juncture, it is important to distinguish between *full* (sometimes called *consistent, radical, or hyper-*) *preterism* and *partial* (sometimes called *moderate*) *preterism*. R. C. Sproul distinguishes between the two as follows: Full preterists see virtually all New Testament eschatology as having been realized already—including the return of Christ, the resurrection, and the final judgment.[11] Moderate preterists believe that the Second Coming of Christ and the bodily resurrection are still

---

10 Kenneth Gentry, Jr., *Before Jerusalem Fell: Dating the Book of Revelation*, 3d ed., (Atlanta: American Vision, 1999). There are several reasons to reject such an early date for the writing of Revelation. For a brief treatment, see Richard Mayhue, "Jesus: A Preterist or Futurist?" Paper presented to the Evangelical Theological Society, Danvers, MA; November, 1999. For a more thorough critique, see Robert Thomas, "Theonomy and the Dating of the Revelation," *The Master's Seminary Journal* 5 (Spring 1994), 185-202; and *Revelation 1-7: An Exegetical Commentary*, (Chicago: Moody Press, 1992), 20-23. Further discussion of the dating of Revelation is beyond the scope of this book.

11 Keith Mathison goes into further detail as he describes the doctrine of full preterists. He says the essential defining doctrine of full preterism is that all eschatological events, such as the Second Coming and the Last Judgment, took place at the destruction of Jerusalem. He then quotes Edward Stevens in listing seventeen propositions that summarize the full preterist position: 1. The kingdom has arrived. 2. The kingdom is spiritual. 3. The kingdom must be entered and dwelt in through spiritual means. 4. All things written about Christ in the Old Testament have been fulfilled (Luke 21:22). 5. The Great Commission has been fulfilled (Matt. 28:18-20). 6. All things have been made new (Rev. 21:5). 7. The scheme of redemption has been consummated. 8. The old heavens and earth have passed away, and the new heavens and earth are here (Matt. 5:17-20). 9. The time of reformation has occurred (Heb. 9:10). 10. Christ has returned. 11. The "perfect" has come (1 Cor. 13:10; Eph. 4:13). 12. The first covenant became obsolete and disappeared (Heb. 8:13). 14. The mystery is finished (Rom. 16:25-26; 1 Cor. 2:6-8; Eph. 3:4-10; Rev. 10:7). 15. Death and hades have been thrown into the lake of fire (Rev. 20:13-14). 16. All things have been "restored" (Acts 3:21). 17. Armageddon is past. Keith Mathison, *Postmillennialism: An Eschatology of Hope*, (Phillipsburg, NJ: P&R Publishing, 1999), 235-36; quoting Edward Stevens, "Doctrinal Implications of Preterist Eschatology," unpublished paper.

future, but agree that the Tribulation period described in the Olivet Discourse, as well as the coming of Christ in Matthew 24:29-31, was fulfilled in the destruction of Jerusalem in A. D. 70.[12] I will limit my discussion to moderate preterism, since full preterism is properly classified as heretical given its departure from orthodox Christianity on so many points.[13]

A full discussion of the many implications of preterism would be a fitting topic for a much longer book, and this present work makes no attempt to give such a discussion. My more modest goal is to examine the preterist interpretation of the Olivet Discourse found in Matthew 24-25. While that method will not answer all the questions raised by preterism, it will allow a discussion of the key principles that underlie preterist thought—particularly its historical, hermeneutical, and exegetical principles. I will explain the preterist view from the writings of its main proponents and then evaluate it in light of Scripture.

A Brief History of Preterism

The first preterist interpretation of the Olivet Discourse is often attributed to Eusebius (263-339) in his *Ecclesiastical History* and *The Proof of the Gospel*.[14] After quoting Josephus' account of the destruction of Jerusalem at length, Eusebius writes:

> All this occurred in this manner, in the second year of the reign of Vespasian [69-79], according to the predictions of our Lord and Saviour Jesus Christ, who by his divine power foresaw all these things as if already present at the

12 Sproul, *The Last Days*, 24, 68, 153-70. Cf. Kenneth Gentry, Jr., "A Brief Theological Analysis of Hyper-Preterism," *Chalcedon Report*, 384 (July 1997) 22-24, in which he declares full preterism to be heterodox and outside the creedal orthodoxy of Christianity.

13 Cf. Gentry, "A Brief Theological Analysis of Hyper-Preterism," 22-24.

14 Thomas Ice, "Back to the Future: Keeping the Future in the Future," in *The Return*, ed. Thomas Ice and Timothy J. Demy, (Grand Rapids: Kregel, 1999), 15.

time, who wept and mourned indeed, at the prospect, as the holy evangelists show in their writings.[15]

Thomas Ice indicates that the first systematic presentation of the preterist viewpoint appeared in 1614 by Alcazar, a Jesuit friar. He influenced the first Protestant preterist, Hugo Grotius of Holland, whose work appeared in 1644. Preterism first appeared in England through a commentary by Henry Hammond in 1653.[16]

Modern preterist writers like Kenneth Gentry claim that a number of well-known scholars from the Reformation to the present are in their camp, including John Calvin (1509-1564), John Lightfoot (1601-1675), John Owen (1616-1683), Matthew Henry (1662-1714), John Gill (1697-1771), Thomas Scott (1747-1821), Adam Clarke (1762-1832), Moses Stuart (1780-1852), J. A. Alexander (1809-1860), Albert Barnes (1798-1870), Philip Schaff (1819-1893), David Brown (1803-1897), F. W. Farrar (1831-1903), Milton Terry (1840-1914), Benjamin B. Warfield (1851-1921), J. Marcellus Kik (1903-1965), and Loraine Boettner (1903-1989).[17]

The paucity of names that Gentry lists from the past century is notable. Indeed, preterism has largely been off the theological radar screen for many years. It did not even merit a separate entry in such standard works as *Baker's Dictionary of Theology* (1960),[18] *Evangelical Dictionary of Theol-*

15 Eusebius, *Ecclesiastical History*, 3.7.1, in *Eusebius' Ecclesiastical History*, translated by Christian Frederick Cruse, (Grand Rapids: Baker, 1981), reprint ed, 93. Gentry believes Origen (185-254) was also a preterist. "The Great Tribulation Is Past," 13.

16 Ice, "Back to the Future," 16.

17 Gentry, "The Great Tribulation Is Past," 13. Verification of his claim is difficult due to his lack of supporting citations. In any event, a full-fledged history of preterism is beyond the scope of the immediate paper. Given its recent rise in prominence, further research on this issue would be valuable, particularly to assess preterism's relationship to the optimistic postmillennialism of the 19th century and to evaluate the extent to which these past scholars would support preterism as it has been developed by its modern proponents.

18 Everett F. Harrison, ed., *Baker's Dictionary of Theology*, (Grand Rapids:

ogy (1984),[19] and *New Dictionary of Theology* (1988).[20] Even the more recent, eschatologically-focused work *Dictionary of Premillennial Theology* (1996) does not have a separate entry for preterism.[21]

As shown below, however, preterism has been making inroads into evangelicalism in the past few years, with several works questioning futuristic views on eschatology. The Olivet Discourse in Matthew 24-25 has received wide discussion in preterist literature, presenting the need to assess the preterist interpretation in greater detail.[22]

Baker, 1960).

19 Walter A. Elwell, ed., *Evangelical Dictionary of Theology*, (Grand Rapids: Baker, 1984).

20 Sinclair B. Ferguson, David F. Wright, and J. I. Packer, eds., *New Dictionary of Theology*, (Downers Grove: InterVarsity Press, 1988). The fact that preterism may have been mentioned in passing as a historical footnote in commentaries on Revelation does not obscure the present point. If, as the preterists claim, their interpretation of the Olivet Discourse is so irrefutably clear, it is surprising that the first two centuries of church history and virtually the entire past century of scholarly work missed the point.

21 Mal Couch, ed. *Dictionary of Premillennial Theology*, (Grand Rapids: Kregel, 1996). This work does make a passing reference to preterism under the entry "Reconstructionism, Christian," by Thomas D. Ice.

22 Page constraints will limit the remaining discussion to a presentation and critique of the preterist view. A defense of the futurist view of the Olivet Discourse is beyond the scope of this paper. For futurist treatments of the Olivet Discourse see Paul Benware, *Understanding End Times Prophecy*, (Chicago: Moody Press, 1995), 317-20; Stanley D. Toussaint, "Are the Church and the Rapture in Matthew 24?", in *The Return*, edited by Thomas Ice and Timothy J. Demy (Grand Rapids: Kregel, 1999), 122-36; and Bruce Ware, "Is the Church in View in Matthew 24-25?", in *Vital Prophetic Issues*, edited by Roy B. Zuck (Grand Rapids: Kregel, 1995), 185-98. For a popular, yet helpful and detailed, treatment, see John MacArthur, *The Second Coming*, (Wheaton: Crossway, 1999).

The Preterist View of the Olivet Discourse

The preterist interpretation of the Olivet Discourse is represented in the writings of R. C. Sproul,[23] Kenneth Gentry,[24] and Gary DeMar.[25] These men have generated substantial literature on the topic, with DeMar's tome on preterism exceeding 500 pages. The volume of this material makes a verse-by-verse review of their entire interpretation impractical for present purposes. Consequently, I will simply outline the basic preterist understanding of the Olivet Discourse and explain their treatment of Matthew 24:34, which they consider to be the key verse in the entire passage. The exegetical effect of that interpretation on the rest of the Discourse will be illustrated with specific examples from other verses.

Jewish Judgment: The Preterist Theme for Matthew's Gospel

The preterist prefaces his interpretation of the Olivet Discourse with an emphasis on the Jewish concern of Matthew's gospel.[26] He notes that it opens with a reference to Jesus' ancestry through David back to Abraham (1:1). He then emphasizes Matthew's presentation of judgment against Israel. John the Baptist calls Israel to repentance for her sin (3:1-2, 6) and rebukes her religious leaders (3:7-9). Israel's lack of faith is contrasted with Jesus' amazement at a Gentile's faith—faith that He did not find with anyone in Israel. Although many will come from east and west and recline with Abraham, Isaac,

23 Sproul, *The Last Days*, 29-48.

24 Gentry, "The Great Tribulation Is Past," 33-66.

25 Gary DeMar, *Last Days Madness*, 3d ed. (Atlanta: American Vision, 1997). DeMar's book is now in its fourth edition (1999). For purposes of this book, DeMar will be considered a partial preterist although he does not distance himself from full preterism in the book.

26 For greater simplicity, Gentry's summary of Matthew's theme will be taken as representative of other preterists with the understanding that preterists may have points of disagreement between themselves on some of the details.

and Jacob, the sons of the kingdom shall be cast out into the outer darkness (8:10-13).[27]

Later, Jesus compares Israel to pagan cities of old (11:16-24), and says that the men of Nineveh and the Queen of the South would stand up with this generation at the judgment and condemn it (12:38-45). Jesus castigates Israel's rulers by saying, "This people honors me with their lips, but their heart is far away from Me" (15:8).[28]

Then, beginning in chapter 21, Matthew starts piling up judgment material. Jesus cleanses the temple of its corrupting influences (21:12-16) and curses the fig tree, indicating the imminent judgment against the nation (21:19-20, 42-45). He castigates Israel's rulers for their long-standing opposition to God's prophets, and indicates that God will withdraw His kingdom from them and bestow it upon a nation producing the fruit of it (21:23-46). Jesus then proclaims the parable of the marriage feast, which recounts Israel's resistance to God's call, and predicts the gathering of other guests (the Gentiles) to the feast (22:1-14).[29]

Chapter 23 then sets the stage for the Olivet Discourse by calling down seven woes upon Israel's religious leaders. God's vengeance will crash down against all those who shed innocent blood in first-century Israel (23:36). Jesus then leaves the temple and pronounces that Israel's house is being left to her desolate (23:37-38). After leaving the temple, Jesus heads for the Mount of Olives (24:1). The disciples ask him the questions that spark the Olivet Discourse: "Tell us, when will these things be? And what will be the sign of Your coming, and of the end of the age (24:3)?"[30]

Consequently, the preterist emphasizes Matthew's theme of judgment on Israel as he prepares to interpret the Olivet Dis-

27 Gentry, "The Great Tribulation is Past," 17-18.

28 Ibid, 19.

29 Ibid, 19-20.

30 Ibid, 20-25. Gentry avoids any mention of Matthew 23:39 and moves directly into Matthew 24. That omission is significant and will be addressed below.

course. God's judgment will bring great tribulation upon the nation, and to the preterist, the timing of that tribulation is found in 24:34: "Truly I say to you, this generation will not pass away until all these things take place."

The preterist insists that Matthew 24:34 is indisputably clear that God's judgment on Israel will occur in the first-century, based on the forty-year length of a biblical generation. Since Jesus was speaking sometime around A. D. 30, fulfillment must have occurred by A. D. 70. The preterist finds that in the Roman army's destruction of Jerusalem in A. D. 70.[31]

Past Judgment: The Preterist Interpretation of Matthew 24:34

Matthew 24:34 says:

> Truly I say to you, this generation will not pass away until all these things take place.

The importance of that verse to preterist interpretation cannot be overstated. Gentry calls it "the key to locating the Great Tribulation in history,"[32] that must be understood as a "nonapocalyptic, nonpoetic, unambiguous, didactic assertion."[33] Combined with Matthew's thematic development, Matthew 24:34 is "alone sufficient to locate the Great Tribulation in the first century."[34] As such, it is the "all-important *key* text" for the preterists' understanding of the Olivet Discourse.[35]

R. C. Sproul is also adamant about the importance of Matthew 24:34. Quoting J. Stuart Russell, he states, "No violence can extort from [it] any other sense than the obvious and

---

31 Ibid, 24-27. "Indisputably clear" occurs at the end of p. 26.
32 Ibid, 26.
33 Ibid, 28.
34 Ibid, 33.
35 Ibid, 65 (emphasis in original).

unambiguous one, viz. that our Lord's second coming would take place within the limits of the existing generation."[36] It is a line around prophecy "so plain and palpable, shutting it wholly within a limit so definite and distinct, that it ought to be decisive of the whole question."[37] Indeed, "99 persons in every 100 would immediately understand Jesus to mean that the events he was predicting would fall within the limits of the lifetime of an existing generation."[38]

Gary DeMar adds, "If Jesus said that all the events prior to Matthew 24:34 would occur before the contemporary generation (within forty years) passed away, then we must take Him at His word. . . An honest assessment of Scripture can lead to no other conclusion. The integrity of the Bible is at stake in the discussion of the biblical meaning of 'this generation.'"[39]

Why do preterists find this interpretation so compelling? Gentry offers a seven-point argument in support of a first-century fulfillment of Matthew 24:4-35:[40]

1. The first-century temple is the focus of the disciples' question (Matt. 24:1-2a).

2. The first-century temple is, in fact, destroyed in Jesus' generation.

36 J. Stuart Russell, *The Parousia: A Critical Inquiry into the New Testament Doctrine of Our Lord's Second Coming*, (Londond: Unwin, 1887), reprint ed. (Grand Rapids: Baker, 1983), 539-40; quoted in Sproul, *The Last Days*, 25.

37 Russell, *The Parousia*, 83-84; quoted in Sproul, *The Last Days*, 47.

38 Sproul, *The Last Days*, 53 (alluding to Russell).

39 DeMar, *Last Days Madness*, 73.

40 Gentry, "The Great Tribulation Is Past," 28-32. It should be noted that Gentry only argues for an A. D. 70 fulfillment of Matthew 24:4-35. He views the rest of the discourse as still future, believing that Jesus begins to look forward to the future in Matthew 24:36. "The Great Tribulation Is Past," 26. I respond in the next chapter under the heading "Does Sound Exegesis Support Preterism?"

3. The warning embedded in the prophecy indicates the primary focus of the events (Matt. 24:16). By telling His followers to flee to the mountains, Jesus was confining the scope of His prophecy.

4. "This generation" indisputably applies to the scribes and Pharisees earlier in the context (Matt. 23:36).

5. The first mention of "generation" in Matthew uses the Greek term in the sense of a life span (Matt. 1:17).

6. "Generation" is used elsewhere in Matthew (and the other gospels) of those living in Christ's day (Matt. 12:38-39; 17:17). (This point is especially important to preterists.)

7. The phrase "this generation" elsewhere in Matthew points to the contemporary generation of Christ's own day (Matt. 11:16; 12:40-45).

These contextual factors drive the preterist to understand "generation" in a manner that will not permit a fulfillment of Jesus' prophecy after the first century. DeMar believes that to take Matthew 24:34 as referring to anything other than Jesus' immediate contemporaries is to violate the way the phrase is used in every other place in Matthew and the New Testament.[41] Sproul, on the other hand, is less adamant. He believes the other uses of "this generation" as referring to Jesus' contemporaries are "weighty," but not conclusive.[42]

Based on that understanding, the preterist proceeds to explain that "all these things" in v. 34 simply refers to everything previously mentioned in Matthew 24:4-33. The "Great Tribulation" of verse 21 describes the events that must occur in "this generation."[43] Sproul adds:

41 DeMar, *Last Days Madness*, 72.

42 Sproul, *The Last Days*, 62.

43 Gentry, "The Tribulation Is Past," 27, 65. Gentry assumes, but does not

If both "this generation" and "all these things" are taken at face value, then either all the content of Jesus' Olivet Discourse, including the *parousia* he describes here, have already taken place (in some sense), or at least some of Jesus' prophecy failed to take place within the time-frame assigned to it.[44]

The preterists generally do little exegesis on the term "shall not pass away." Gentry only notes that the phrase has an emphatic double negative (οὐ μή). Since a generation was reckoned as forty years in the Old Testament, Jesus was insisting that the events of 24:4-33 would occur within forty years.[45] In effect, the preterist looks ahead to Matthew 24:34 as he is reading the chapter, and then retroactively applies it to the interpretation of the preceding section. The effect of that interpretive method now follows.

Preterist Interpretation of Other Texts in Matthew 24

One question unlocks the preterist view. How can he claim past fulfillment of the Olivet Discourse, when so much of its language seems to refer to the future?

The preterist's understanding of Matthew 24:34 is the presupposition that determines the timing of the fulfillment of Matthew 24:4-33. The preterist allows nothing to contradict that preunderstanding he brings to the text.

Consequently, when the ordinary sense of other texts in

---

prove, that the antecedent of "all these things" is the entire discourse from 24:4-34.

44 Sproul, *The Last Days*, 64-65. Sproul equivocates on what remains future in his understanding of preterism: "I must confess that I am still unsettled on some crucial matters. I am convinced that the substance of the Olivet Discourse was fulfilled in A. D. 70 and that the bulk of Revelation was likewise fulfilled in that time-frame. I share Gentry's concerns about full preterism, particularly on such issues as the consummation of the kingdom and the resurrection of the dead." Ibid., 158.

45 Gentry, "The Great Tribulation Is Past," 27.

Matthew 24 seems to refer to events still future today, the preterist reinterprets them by using figurative language to refer to
a now-past event. Biblical cross-references are used to support
the figurative interpretation. He then buttresses his view with
citations to ancient historians (especially Josephus) to lend
credibility to the figurative interpretation of past fulfillment.
To illustrate that methodology, the preterist interpretation of
Matthew 24:15-18 and Matthew 24:29-31 will now be exam-
ined.

Matthew 24:15-18
In this text, Jesus spoke about the abomination of desolation
found in Daniel 9:26-27:

> Therefore when you see the abomination of desolation
> which was spoken of through Daniel the prophet,
> standing in the holy place (let the reader understand),
> then those who are in Judea must flee to the mountains.
> Whoever is on the housetop must not go down to get the
> things out that are in his house. Whoever is in the field
> must not turn back to get his cloak. (Matt. 24:15-18)

The preterist says that the "abomination of desolation"
refers not to an individual, but rather to an abuse of worship
in the Jerusalem temple that occurred during the Roman siege
of Jerusalem. Gentry writes:

> During the Roman siege, the Zealots hole up in Jerusalem,
> and stir up factional infighting between the parties
> of John of Gischala, Eleazar, and Simon. Even while
> Jerusalem's mighty walls resist the Romans, this internal
> strife brings war into the holy temple itself.[46]

Gentry then quotes Josephus, who recorded that the Jewish
in-fighting was so bad that 8500 people perished in the conflict.
The Zealots went through the temple and used the sacred wine

46 Ibid, 47.

and distributed it to the people. But even beyond the Zealots, the preterist sees fulfillment in the Roman soldiers, whose ensigns of eagles violated Jewish sensibilities about images. Their presence in a time of war would be an abomination (i.e., the ensigns of eagles) leading to "desolation" (i.e., the destruction of the temple).[47]

Preterists believe that after Jesus gave this prediction about the coming destruction of Jerusalem, He proceeded to advise the Christians in Judea to flee to the mountains for safety when they saw the Roman army beginning to surround Jerusalem (24:16-18). Preterists sprinkle Josephus' descriptions of Roman troop movements during the siege throughout their exposition to lend historical authenticity to this interpretation. Gentry concludes: "In A. D. 70, the Roman "eagles" gather over the corpse of Jerusalem to pick it clean (24:28)."[48]

Matthew 24:29-31
Another helpful illustration of the preterist interpretive methodology can be found in this text.

> But immediately after the tribulation of those days the sun will be darkened, and the moon will not give its light, and the stars will fall from the sky, and the powers of the heavens will be shaken. And then the sign of the Son of Man will appear in the sky, and then all the tribes of the earth will mourn, and they will see the Son of Man coming on the clouds of the sky with power and great glory. And He will send forth His angels with a great trumpet and they will gather together His elect from the four winds, from one end of the sky to the other. (Matt. 24:29-31)

By their own admission, this is a difficult passage for preterists to interpret. The cosmic disturbances seem too catastrophic to apply to A. D. 70. However, Gentry sidesteps the difficulty by

47 Ibid, 47-48; cf. Sproul, *The Last Days*, 39-41.
48 Gentry, "The Great Tribulation Is Past," 48-50.

appealing to a figurative interpretation. He says the verses must be interpreted *"covenantally,* which is to say *biblically,* rather than according to a presupposed simple literalism."[49]

Gentry argues that the apocalyptic language of Matthew 24:29-31 is a dramatic way of expressing national calamity. He quotes Isaiah's prophecy of judgment against Babylon in Isaiah 13:10, 13 in support: "For the stars of heaven and their constellations will not flash forth their light; the sun will be dark when it rises and the moon will not shed its light. . . . Therefore I will make the heavens tremble, and the earth will be shaken from its place." He adds Ezekiel 32:2, 7-8; Jeremiah 4:11, 23-24, 29; and Joel 2:1, 10 to his list of illustrations.[50]

Based on those Old Testament examples, the preterist argues that Christ's use of similar imagery in Matthew 24:29 should be understood the same way. Jesus is not literally speaking about an upheaval of the heavens; He is using poetic language to describe the impending destruction of Jerusalem. "In a sense, it is 'the end of the world' for those nations God judges. So is it with Israel in A. D. 70: her time of God's favor ends, and her temple system vanishes from history."[51]

But what about Matthew 24:30, which speaks of the sign of the Son of Man appearing in the sky? Gentry further argues that the NASB has inaccurately translated οὐρανός as "sky." Instead, it should be understood as "heaven." The temple's final destruction is the sign that the Son of Man is in heaven, God's racial focus on Israel has ended, the land promises are over, and the typological ministry is fading away.[52]

The preterist then asserts that this "sign" was not a world-wide phenomenon. He says the "tribes of the earth" (πᾶσαι αἱ φυλαὶ τῆς γῆς) refers not to all people everywhere but to "the tribes of the land"—i.e., the twelve tribes of Israel.[53]

49 Ibid, 55 (emphasis in original).
50 Ibid, 55-56.
51 Ibid, 56-57.
52 Ibid, 58-59.
53 Ibid, 59-60.

By now, it has all become convoluted to follow. According to the preterist, Jesus was not describing a celestial event for all to see. He was actually referring to His ascension. There is no need for a visual sign in the skies over all the earth, for the sign was only to Israel.

Further, the "coming" described in v. 30 is not a physical coming, but rather a sign that the destruction of Jerusalem proved that Christ is now the ascended Lord who has great power and glory.[54]

One might wonder how the first-century Jews were supposed to *see* this judgment if Christ was in heaven beyond the reach of human eyes. The preterist argues that the "seeing" in Matthew 24:30 does not occur with the organ of vision. Instead, the Jews would *understand* (as we "see" the solution to a math problem) that the temple destruction is proof of Jesus' judgment against Israel."[55] With the Old Covenant system destroyed, the "angels" were now free to gather the elect from one end of the sky to another (24:31)—which refers to the freedom human messengers now have to preach the gospel from horizon to horizon and bring the elect into the kingdom of God.[56]

---

54 Ibid, 57, 60-61.

55 Ibid, 60.

56 Ibid, 64. The careful reader will note the different interpretations the preterist gives to the various forms of οὐρανός, which occur five times in these three verses. In verse 29, it refers to the skies which contain the heavenly bodies (Gentry, 55-57; referring metaphorically to God's judgment). In verse 30, it refers to God's heavenly throne room to which Christ ascended (Gentry, 58). In verse 31, it refers to the earth, representing the four corners of the globe from which the elect are gathered. Preterists make the same term in the same context mean wildly different things. That exegetical inconsistency is merely one of the fatal weaknesses found in preterism.

Summary

While these passages from Matthew 24:34, 24:15-18, and 24:29-31 do not exhaust the preterist interpretation of the Olivet Discourse, they are more than sufficient to illustrate how preterists reach their conclusions. The interpretation of Matthew 24:34 demands a first-century fulfillment of everything that precedes it. Those passages that would seem to be still future in fulfillment are interpreted figuratively to apply to events in A. D. 70. Once the figurative interpretation has been established, it is supported with citations from ancient historians.

5

An Evaluation
of Preterism

For I say to you, from now on you will not see Me until you say,
"Blessed is He who comes in the name of the Lord."
(Matthew 23:39)

Does History Support Preterism?

For a movement that prides itself on its historical knowledge and accuracy, preterism has historical embarrassments that preclude it from being a viable eschatological option. As mentioned previously, the preterist believes that Matthew 24:29-31 indicates that the people of that day will understand that Christ had come in judgment when Jerusalem was destroyed in A. D. 70.[57] The significance would be so apparent that no one could miss it—and that would presumably be even more true for believers who embraced the words of Christ.

But early church writings contemporaneous with A. D. 70, show that the writers *of that very era* understood Jesus' words in a futuristic sense. They contradict the preterists' allegation that Jesus was speaking of the destruction of Jerusalem.[58] The *Didache*, for example, which probably dates in its present form from the end of the first century to no later than A. D. 150, clearly anticipated a *future* fulfillment of the Olivet Discourse. Due to its historical significance on this point, it will be quoted at length here:

57 Gentry, "The Great Tribulation Is Past," 60-61.

58 Cf. John MacArthur, *The Second Coming*, (Wheaton: Crossway, 1999), 123-24; Richard Mayhue, "Jesus: A Preterist or Futurist?" 20-21.

[3] For in the last days the false prophets and corrupters will abound, and the sheep will be turned into wolves, and love will be turned into hate. [4] For as lawlessness increases, they will hate and persecute and betray one another. And then the deceiver of the world will appear as a son of God and "will perform signs and wonders," and the earth will be delivered into his hands, and he will commit abominations the likes of which have never happened before. [5] Then all humankind will come to the fiery test, and "many will fall away" and perish; but "those who endure" in their faith "will be saved" by the accursed one himself. [6] And "then there will appear the signs" of the truth: first the sign of an opening in heaven, then the sign of the sound of a trumpet, and third, the resurrection of the dead—[7] but not of all; rather, as it has been said, "The Lord will come, and all his saints with him." [8] Then the world "will see the Lord coming upon the clouds of heaven."[59]

The *Didache* plainly anticipates a future fulfillment of the Olivet Discourse. The writer(s) believed that, in the future, the heavens would open, the trumpet would sound, the dead would be resurrected, and *then* the *world* would see the Lord coming upon the clouds of heaven. No mention is made of the destruction of Jerusalem, but rather a world-wide event that follows the resurrection of the dead. That is utterly inconceivable if, as the preterists claim, the cloud-coming of Jesus would be so obviously a final judgment of Jerusalem that no one could miss it.

The dating of the *Didache* is significant for another reason as well. While the present form (quoted above) is dated before A. D. 150, it is based on materials composed at an earlier time—perhaps as early as A.D. 70.[60] The original materials,

---

59 *Didache* 16:3-8. In J. B. Lightfoot and J.R. Harmer, editors and translators, *The Apostolic Fathers,* 2d ed., edited and revised by Michael W. Holmes (Grand Rapids: Baker, 1991), 158.

60 Lightfoot, *The Apostolic Fathers,* 146.

then, were virtually contemporaneous with the destruction of Jerusalem, and do not see that event as the fulfillment of the Olivet Discourse. Subsequent compilers, who would have had opportunity to correct that portion of the document if they deemed it incorrect, instead retained the interpretation.

Nor is this argument limited to the *Didache*. Justin Martyr (c. A. D. 140-150) wrote in his "Dialogue with Trypho" the following:

> Two advents of Christ have been announced: the one, in which He is set forth as suffering, inglorious, dishonoured, and crucified; but the other, in which He shall come from heaven with glory, when the man of apostasy, who speaks strange things against the Most High, shall venture to do unlawful deeds on the earth against us the Christians. . . the rest of the prophecy shall be fulfilled at His second coming.[61]

That proves those who were in the church during the apostolic age, and were contemporaries of the destruction of Jerusalem, were not preterists. If the preterist interpretation were true, the earliest church fathers missed (1) what Jesus said they could not miss; and (2) what preterists today claim is "indisputably clear."

The historical facts contradict preterism and are a fatal weakness in the preterist scheme.[62]

61 Justin Martyr, "Dialogue with Trypho," chap. 110; in *The Ante-Nicene Fathers*, ed. Alexander Roberts and James Donaldson. Vol. 1. Grand Rapids: Eerdmans, 1969 reprint, 253-54. For further discussion with additional examples, see J. N. D. Kelly, *Early Christian Doctrines*, rev. ed. (San Francisco: Harper & Row, 1978), 459-69.

62 One might argue that the church fathers were not inspired writers, and therefore the modern reader does not have to accept their interpretation. The issue is not whether their interpretation of Scripture is correct, but whether their understanding of their day comports with what preterists insist it must have been. If Jesus' statement about "this generation" was so "indisputably clear" that "no one could miss it," why did the church look for future fulfillment of the Olivet Discourse after they had witnessed the destruction of Jerusalem?

More than church history speaks against the historical accuracy of the preterist position. Josephus' description of the fall of Jerusalem does not square with a careful reading of the Olivet Discourse, either. Neil Nelson lists nine reasons why it is unlikely that Matthew 24:15-28 refers to the events of A.D. 70:

1. A.D. 70 was not "great tribulation such as has not been from the beginning of the world until now, no, and never will be" (Matt. 24:21).

2. Matthew declares that the abomination came first, followed by the great tribulation and flight. The abomination causes the desolation. In the siege of Titus, however, the tribulation preceded the abomination.

3. The abomination of desolation takes place "in the holy place," which is probably the Jewish temple (cf. Acts 6:13; 21:28). In Daniel the abomination is always linked to the temple. When the Roman standards stood in the temple it was too late for flight into the mountains.

4. If the elect are Christians who escaped to Pella, what need was there for shortening those days?

5. There is little historical evidence for false Christs appearing around the time of the Jewish war or for false Christs performing great miracles.

6. A.D. 70 did not drive masses of professing Christians to apostatize.

7. Every human being would not have been destroyed by the Jewish war (Matt. 24:22) Would all Roman soldiers have been killed?

8. Matthew 24:29 states that the *parousia* (24:29-31) comes immediately after those days (24:15-28).

9. Matthew 24:14 speaks of the absolute end. Matthew 24:15 is connected by οὖν to the preceding verses. It is natural for 24:15-28 to describe the same general period.[63]

Normally, historical arguments are not decisive in choosing between interpretive options. But in this case, the preterists have backed themselves into a corner from which they cannot escape. They insist that those who lived in A. D. 70 would have understood that the destruction of Jerusalem meant that Jesus had come in judgment. Yet those closest to the destruction of Jerusalem embraced the very futurism that the preterists reject. Those who should be the preterists' most potent allies— those closest to A.D. 70—utterly repudiate preterist doctrine.

Early church writings are another fatal weakness in the preterist scheme.

Do Sound Hermeneutics Support Preterism?

To embark on a comprehensive discussion of the interpretation of prophecy at this juncture would be to dive into a deep well with full knowledge of the impossibility of escape. The vast literature and numerous opinions on the subject stretch far beyond the scope of this book.[64]

All would agree that the Olivet Discourse presents many interpretive challenges no matter the eschatological position of the interpreter. R. C. Sproul proposes three basic solutions to those problems:

63 Neil D. Nelson, Jr., " 'This Generation' in Matt 24:34: A Literary Critical Perspective," *Journal of the Evangelical Theological Society* 38 (September 1996) 379-80, n. 33.

64 For a brief survey of the issues, see John F. Walvoord, "Basic Considerations in Interpreting Prophecy," in *Vital Prophetic Issues*, edited by Roy B. Zuck (Grand Rapids: Kregel, 1995), 14-22.

1. We can interpret the entire discourse literally. In this case we must conclude that some elements of Jesus' prophecy failed to come to pass.

2. We can interpret the events surrounding the predicted parousia literally and interpret the time-frame references figuratively. This method is employed chiefly by those who do not restrict the phrase "this generation will not pass away" to the life span of Jesus' contemporaries.

3. We can interpret the time-frame references literally and the events surrounding the parousia figuratively. In this view, all of Jesus' prophecies in the Olivet Discourse were fulfilled during the period of the discourse itself and the destruction of Jerusalem in A.D. 70.[65]

Sproul says that, when faced with the choice between a literal interpretation of the time references and a literal description of the parousia, the preterist "chooses" the former, based on the larger hermeneutical principle of the analogy of Scripture.[66] Sproul sees that a consistent literalism would undermine the entire preterist scheme. In other words, the preterist acknowledges that he is literal in some places but figurative in others.

By contrast, one of the standard authors on biblical interpretation sees the situation differently. Bernard Ramm, in his extensive discussion on the interpretation of prophecy, says, "The interpreter should take the literal meaning of a prophetic passage as his limiting or controlling guide."[67] Without denying the presence of figures of speech or symbols, Ramm emphasizes that the literal meaning of words cannot be aban-

65 Sproul, *The Last Days*, 66.

66 Ibid.

67 Bernard Ramm, *Protestant Biblical Interpretation*, 3d rev. ed. (Grand Rapids: Baker, 1973), 253-54.

doned simply because the interpreter is handling prophetic literature.

What the preterist does is devastating to a clear understanding of the text. For example, Gentry assigns at least three contradictory meanings to οὐρανός in his interpretation of Matthew 24:29-31.[68] He can say that the same word means "horizon," "sky," and "heavenly throne room" in the same context only because he has abandoned the literal meaning of the term. He must find a symbolic meaning to fit the need of the moment or his entire scheme will collapse. Once the preterist makes that choice, the "sky is the limit" for imaginative interpretations that have no bearing on the original intent of Jesus' words.[69]

The preterist might respond to that charge by saying he provides biblical examples for his symbolic interpretations. One can grant that without diminishing the force of the critique. The importation of verses from other scriptural contexts does not alter the significance of his interpretive error. D. A. Carson refers to this practice as the unwarranted "juxtaposition of texts," and asks:

> What gives interpreters the right to link certain verses together, and not others? The point is that all such linking eventually produces a grid that affects the interpretation of other texts. There may be fallacies connected not only with the way individual verses are interpreted, but also with the way several passages are linked—and then also with the way such a link affects the interpretation of the next verse that is studied![70]

The careful student, once sensitive to this issue, will immediately see how this "exegetical fallacy" characterizes virtually every page of preterist writings. The quoting of verses simply

68 See footnote 53 for details.

69 Pun intended.

70 D. A. Carson, *Exegetical Fallacies*, 2d ed., (Grand Rapids: Baker, 1996), 139.

to demonstrate a vague verbal parallel by itself does not establish the proper interpretation of any passages, and further does not constitute "letting Scripture interpret Scripture." Such loose cross-referencing only reflects the interpreter's bias.

Similarly, preterists err in their interpretation of the Olivet Discourse when they allow Matthew 24:34 to dominate their interpretation of other verses in the passage. The persuasiveness of the preterist interpretation of the Olivet Discourse depends on the interpreter's ability to establish that Matthew 24:34 demands a first century fulfillment. The preterist must establish that premise before he even begins his verse-by-verse exposition of Matthew 24.[71]

For example, Gentry insists that Matthew 24:21-22, which predicts a great tribulation that will surpass all other tribulations for all of time, must refer to the destruction of Jerusalem in A. D. 70. Why? Gentry leaps over twelve verses to discuss "this generation" in 24:34. Since "this generation" is "obviously" a literal time reference, then Matthew 24:21-22 must be interpreted symbolically to refer to the destruction of Jerusalem. That interpretation, Gentry admits, would not be allowed if Matthew 24:21-22 were interpreted literally. Thus, by fiat of the interpreter, Matthew 24:34 determines the meaning of 24:21-22.[72]

A similar hermeneutical error occurs in Gentry's interpretation of Matthew 24:29, which predicts cosmic disturbances on a grand scale before the coming of Christ. Can the reader take that verse literally to refer to disturbances in the heavenly bodies? Gentry says no. Such cosmic disturbances are too catastrophic to fit into what we know about A.D. 70, and that would not fit with a "literal" interpretation of Matthew 24:34.[73]

---

71 Gentry establishes his interpretation of Matthew 24:34 on pages 26-32 of "The Great Tribulation is Past;" his exposition of Matthew 24 begins on page 33. Sproul discusses the time frame references on pages 15-17 of *The Last Days According to Jesus*; his exposition of the Olivet Discourse begins on page 29. Gary DeMar first gives his interpretation of Matthew 24:34 on page 3 of *Last Days Madness* (then quotes the verse 33 times thereafter).

72 See Gentry, 51.

73 Gentry, 55.

Gentry then proceeds to assert that the cosmic disturbances are not really cosmic disturbances, but merely apocalyptic language to express national calamity or disturbance. He juxtaposes Isaiah 40:26 in support of his position. Matthew 24:34 simply requires 24:29 to be interpreted differently than a plain reading would allow.[74] In yet another passage, he speaks of Matthew 24:34 "controlling" Matthew 24:30.[75]

Through these examples, the reader should see that a preterist filters the entire Olivet Discourse through the grid of his understanding of 24:34. That verse is his interpretive starting point. The preterist cannot interpret the rest of the Olivet Discourse *in the same way* he interprets 24:34 because otherwise he will end up with passages that forbid the A. D. 70 date. This is a serious interpretive error, which, if followed throughout Scripture, would irretrievably obscure the clarity of God's Word.

The correct hermeneutical approach allows each text equal weight in the interpretive process. Since all Scripture is equally inspired by God (cf. 2 Tim. 3:16-17), each text should be allowed to speak on its own without being "controlled" by another text chosen by the interpreter. Only then can the full measure of God's revelation be brought to bear on the interpretive task.

An approach that allows one verse to dominate all others— to the point of contradicting the clear sense of the subjugated verses—simply reflects the interpreter's bias. It is arbitrary and theologically self-serving. Such is the case with preterism's elevation of Matthew 24:34 in the Olivet Discourse.[76]

Robert Thomas insightfully writes: "Preterism follows

74 Ibid.

75 Gentry, "Conclusion," 195.

76 In this regard, preterists follow a hermeneutical principle similar to evangelical feminists, who use Galatians 3:28 to control the interpretation of all other passages related to women in church leadership. Both preterists and evangelical feminists fail to let each text have equal weight in developing a biblical theology for their respective fields of interest. Cf. Paul Felix, "The Hermeneutics of Evangelical Feminism," *The Master's Seminary Journal* 5 (Fall 1994) 159-84.

a mixture of hermeneutical principles—sometimes literal, sometimes symbolic. . . . That type of interpretive vacillation is the only way one can arrive at a preterist view."[77] Any hermeneutical consistency—whether consistently literal or consistently symbolic—would desolate the preterist system.

Unsound hermeneutics are yet another fatal weakness in the preterist scheme.

Does Sound Exegesis Support Preterism?

Having addressed the historical and hermeneutical problems inherent in preterism, attention must now turn to an exegetical evaluation of its assertions. Once again, only selected passages can be addressed due to space constraints. But the following discussion will be sufficient to prove that preterism cannot withstand exegetical scrutiny.

Matthew 24:34

If a reader only consulted preterist writings, he would have no idea that established scholars from many persuasions do not consider the phrase "this generation" to be "indisputably clear." To the contrary, one commentator wrote that it is "the most difficult phrase to interpret in this complicated eschatological discourse."[78]

The difficulty in interpretation is reflected in the fact that no fewer than eight interpretations of "this generation" have been offered throughout church history. Richard Mayhue surveys eight views that have been held at different times (see his article for supporting citations):

---

77 Robert Thomas, "A Classical Dispensationalist View of Revelation," in *Four Views on the Book of Revelation*, ed. C. Marvin Pate (Grand Rapids: Zondervan, 1998), 213.

78 Joseph A. Fitzmyer, *The Gospel According to Luke (X-XXIV)*, in The Anchor Bible Commentaries, (Garden City, New York: Doubleday, 1985), 1353.

1. Christ was mistaken. This is the majority liberal view.

2. Christ was speaking of the human race in general. This was the secondary view of Jerome regarding Matthew 24:34.

3. Christ was speaking of A.D. 70 alone. This is or has been held by Bruce, Wenham, Beasley-Murray, Plummer, Hagner, Gentry, Carson, Wessel, Sproul, Russell, and DeMar.

4. Christ was implying a preterist/futurist double fulfillment (Carson, Turner).

5. Christ was speaking of faithful Christians in general (Chrysostom).

6. Christ was referring to the Jewish race (futurist view). This was Jerome's primary view, as well as Archer's, Dunham's, Hendriksen's, and Liefeld's.

7. Christ was referring to an eschatological generation (futurist view). This is the normal, but not unanimous, view held by dispensationalists like Walvoord, Blomberg, Liefeld (possibility), Hiebert, Bock, and MacArthur. Archer acknowledges it.

8. Christ was referring to an evil generation (futurist view). This view is held by Alford (historic premillennialist), LaRondelle, Nelson, Thomas, Lenski (amillennialist), Morganthaler, and Lovenstam.[79]

A full-scale solution of this interpretive problem is beyond the scope of this book. However, the briefest acquaintance with the many views—most of which are held by several inter-

79 Mayhue, "Jesus: A Preterist or Futurist?", 16-21.

preters—should dispel preterism's irresponsibly brash assertion that the phrase is "indisputably clear." Preterists have sacrificed their credibility by making such sweeping statements without a meaningful interaction with opposing views.

Neil Nelson has persuasively argued that "generation" refers to an evil kind of people in Matthew's gospel. Nelson acknowledges Jesus' contemporaries are usually in view in Matthew's use of "this generation," but he points out that the references can be more than chronological—they are often *ethical*. Jesus was speaking about *evil, faithless* people when he used the term "generation." That can clearly be seen in passages like 11:16-19; 12:39-41, 45; 16:4, and 17:17.[80] Mayhue adds that γενεά ("generation") refers to "the category of rebellious people who have rejected God's truth and righteousness through the ages."[81]

Not only have preterists failed to acknowledge the ethical dimension to Matthew's use of "generation," but they have also failed to recognize that he uses "this generation" in a way that extends beyond the immediate contemporaries of Jesus. The individuals addressed by "this generation" in Matthew 23:34-36 did not kill Abel nor Zechariah, yet Jesus attributes the murder to them. Nelson writes:

> The contemporaries of Christ did not murder Zechariah son of Berechiah (23:35-36), and thus "this generation" in 23:36 extends beyond Jesus' contemporaries to include murderers back to the time of Abel and forward to those who would kill and crucify and persecute disciples until Jesus returns.[82]

When those factors are combined with the overall futuristic context of the Olivet Discourse, including the Son of Man coming in His glory (24:30; 25:31), sitting on His glorious throne (25:31); and all nations being gathered before Him

80 Nelson, "This Generation," 381, n. 37.

81 Mayhue, "Jesus: A Preterist or Futurist?", 19.

82 Nelson, "This Generation," 381, n. 37.

(25:32), the interpreter has ample reason to understand "this generation" in Matthew 24:34 as referring to the evil generation that will be alive when "all these things take place"—in the future.

Matthew 23:39

Preterists determinedly avoid any significant discussion of Matthew 23:39, where Jesus says to the Jews:

> For I say to you, from now on you shall not see Me until you say, "Blessed is He who comes in the name of the Lord!"

This verse creates another unsolvable dilemma for preterists in light of their interpretation of Matthew 24:30. As shown above, preterists maintain that Matthew 24:30 does not refer to physical sight, but to the Jews' mental understanding that the Lord was judging them for their rejection of Him.

That interpretation cannot possibly be reconciled with 23:39, which says that Israel would not see Jesus again until they joyfully received Him as Messiah. Since the Jews did not receive Jesus as Messiah in A. D. 70, they could not have seen Him then—whether with their physical sight or their mental understanding. Consequently, Matthew 24:30 must still be future—another fatal blow to preterism.[83]

Preterists are aware of this dilemma, but they are not forthright in dealing with it. Gentry devotes nearly two full pages to the significance of Matthew 23:37-38, and then discusses Jesus' departure from the temple in 24:1. He does not even give a verse reference for 23:39 anywhere in his main text.[84]

83 Stanley D. Toussaint, "A Critique of the Preterist View of the Olivet Discourse," unpublished paper presented to the Pre-Trib Study Group, (Dallas: 1996), 4. Cf. Thomas, "A Classical Dispensationalist View of Revelation," 228: "[The Jewish nation] did not at that time say, "Blessed is he who comes in the name of the Lord," so they obviously did not see Jesus at that time. The fulfillment of that prophecy is yet future."

84 Gentry, 23-24. He follows the same pattern elsewhere in the book at pages 172 and 182.

An uninformed reader would not even know Matthew 23:39 existed. Gentry's omission of this verse is palpable, because it critically damages his entire thesis that Christ returned in A.D. 70.

Gentry only mentions the verse in an obscure footnote that is connected to 1 Kings 9:6-9 in the main text. Gentry claims that the phrase, "until you say" suggests an indefinite possibility that may not happen. In other words, the Jews would not see Him again, for they do not so proclaim Him.[85] But that directly contradicts his statement that the Jews *did* see Jesus when He came against them in judgment. He wants to have it both ways. He cannot.

But not only that, Gentry's assertion that "*until* you say" refers to an indefinite possibility is demonstrably false.[86]

Matthew 23:39 indicates that Israel will see Christ when she receives Him as her Messiah. That future event is certain to happen based on the rich Old Testament promises God made to His people (cf. Zech. 12:10).

That conclusion is supported by examining other New Testament uses of ἕως ἄν with the aorist subjunctive ("until"). The following discussion is rather technical, but it is necessary to show that the future contingency of Matthew 23:39 will be fulfilled (all italics supplied):

- Matthew 2:13: Take the Child and His mother and flee to Egypt, and remain there *until I tell* you. . .
- Matthew 5:18: For truly I say to you, *until heaven and earth pass away*, not the smallest letter or stroke shall pass away from the Law, *until all is accomplished*.[87]
- Matthew 10:11: And whatever city or village you enter,

85 Gentry, 208, n. 46. DeMar joins Gentry in this assertion. *Last Days Madness*, 77. Their assertion is not based on independent exegesis, but rather in reliance on R. T. France, *Matthew*, in Tyndale New Testament Commentaries, (Grand Rapids: Eerdmans, 1985), 332.

86 The operative phrase is ἕως ἄν εἴπητε "until you say."

87 This verse is particularly important to theonomic postmillennialists. One wonders if they would consider interpreting it as an "indefinite possibility."

inquire who is worthy in it; and stay at his house *until you leave that city.*

- Matthew 12:20: A battered reed He will not break off, and a smoldering wick He will not put out, *until He leads* justice to victory.
- Matthew 16:28: Truly I say to you, there are some of those who are standing here who will not taste death *until they see* the Son of Man coming in His kingdom.[88]
- Matthew 22:44: The LORD said to my Lord, "Sit at My right hand, *until I put* Your enemies beneath Your feet."[89]
- Matthew 24:34: Truly I say to you, this generation will not pass away *until all these things take place.*
- 1 Corinthians 4:5: Therefore do not go on passing judgment before the time, but wait *until the Lord comes.*

The foregoing verses conclusively establish that the New Testament use of ἕως ἄν ("until") does not refer to an "indefinite possibility." It refers to a future event that will certainly occur, but at a time yet to be determined. To take it as an "indefinite possibility," as preterists suggest, is to cast doubt on such central themes as Christ's fulfillment of the Law (Matthew 5:18), His triumph over His enemies (Matthew 22:44), and His return to earth (1 Corinthians 4:5).

Indeed, to follow the preterists' suggestion on Matthew 23:39 would even undermine their key text of Matthew 24:34: "Truly I say to you, this generation will not pass away *until all these things take place.*" That very verse uses ἕως ἄν with the subjunctive mood. So is Matthew 24:34 a dogmatic certainty, as the preterists state in their exposition of the text, or is it an "indefinite possibility" based on the way they interpret the very same grammar in Matthew 23:39?

The preterist is fatally inconsistent. The brazen self-contradiction at such a determinative point is a sad embarrassment

---

88 Note the identical construction in the parallel passages Mark 9:1 and Luke 9:27 .

89 Note the identical construction in the parallel passages Mark 12:36, Luke 20:43, Acts 2:35, and Hebrews 1:13.

to men who claim to teach the Word of God with care.

Unsound exegesis is yet another fatal weakness in the preterist scheme.

Other Exegetical Considerations

Other exegetical considerations make the preterist interpretation unsatisfying as well. An extended discussion of these points is beyond the scope of this book, yet they should be mentioned to identify additional areas for further study.

First, the preterists do not satisfactorily deal with the concept of the "coming" of Christ in the Olivet Discourse. The Olivet Discourse refers to the coming of the Lord nine times (cf. Matt. 24:3, 27, 30, 37, 39, 42, 43, 44, 48). Gentry considers 24:27 and 24:30 to have been fulfilled in A. D. 70.[90] Yet he views all the references after Matthew 24:36 to be references to the still-future Second Advent.[91] The exegetical base for this distinction (the difference between "this" in Matthew 24:34 and "that" in Matthew 24:36) is flimsy at best. It makes better sense to understand "coming" consistently throughout the discourse.

Second, preterists fail to give adequate consideration to Matthew 24:36:

> But of that day and hour no one knows, not even the angels of heaven, nor the Son, but the Father alone.

Jesus disclaimed knowledge of the timing of future events, and went further to say that *no one* knows. Putting aside the preterists' false distinction between the "cloud-coming" in 24:30 and the other "coming" passages in the Discourse, is it not obvious that the *last* thing Jesus was giving His disciples in the Olivet Discourse was a method to pinpoint the time of His return? Anthony Hoekema comments:

90 Gentry, "The Great Tribulation Is Past," 53, 57-59.
91 Ibid, 26.

If these words mean anything at all, they mean that Christ himself did not know the day or the hour of his return. . . . If, then, Christ himself, according to his own admission, did not know the hour of his return, no other statements of his can be interpreted as indicating the exact time of that return. . . . The insistence that these passages require a Parousia within the generation of those who were contemporaries of Jesus is clearly at variance with Jesus' own disavowal of the knowledge of the time of his return.[92]

Hoekema's counsel is sound. One could add that Jesus' admonition that "no one knows" the day and hour of His return comes *immediately* on the heels of His statement in Matthew 24:34. The preterists must violently violate context to say that 24:36 has no bearing on 24:34. In that regard, it is most convenient that Gentry's exposition stops at 24:35.[93]

Preterists pit themselves against the Lord's own words that no one would know the time of His return. Christ says that no one knows the time. Preterists say they do. It is not difficult to side with our Lord against them.

These additional exegetical considerations are yet another fatal weakness in the preterist scheme.

92 Anthony Hoekema, *The Bible and the Future*, (Grand Rapids: Eerdmans, 1991 reprint ed.), 113.

93 Gentry asserts that the difference between "this" generation in 24:34 and "that" day and hour in 24:36 shows that Jesus was distinguishing between what would be fulfilled in A. D. 70 (i.e., Matthew 24:4-33) and what would be fulfilled in the more distant future (Matthew 24:36-25:46). His argument is unpersuasive. If Jesus was making such a sharp (and critical) disjunction at that point in the discourse, one would expect to find the strong adversative ἀλλά introducing the contrast instead of δέ.

6

Some Brief Reflections on Preterism

But examine everything carefully;
hold fast to that which is good
(1 Thessalonians 5:21)

The Apologetic Concerns of Preterists

In assessing preterism, it is helpful to realize that apologetic concerns are often at the front of their thinking. Preterists are intensely critical of the writings of futurists in past years who used then-current events to speculate on possible dates for the return of Christ to earth. Gary DeMar introduces his book with criticism of writers like Hal Lindsey, Lester Sumrall, Grant Jeffrey, and others who have predicted (with varying degrees of qualification) the date of the return of Christ. As the predicted dates come and go without incident, Christian writers increasingly appear like the little boy who cried "wolf" too many times, with the result that the cause of Christ is harmed before a watching world.[94] Kenneth Gentry has similarly chafed at several prophecy books with titles like *Planet Earth—2000: Will Mankind Survive?; Earth's Final Days; Prophecy 2000: Rushing to Armageddon;* and *Is This the Last Century?*[95]

In addition to the apologetic embarrassment caused by modern-day date-setters, preterists are concerned about the perceived apologetic threat of unfulfilled prophecy. If Matthew 24:34 predicts a first-century fulfillment of Jesus' words, and yet many of Jesus' sayings in the Olivet Discourse remain unfulfilled, the door is open for critics to assert that He was mistaken about the timing of His return. And if Jesus was mis-

94 DeMar, *Last Days Madness*, 1-21.
95 Gentry, "The Great Tribulation Is Past," 11.

taken, the Bible loses its authority, and the gospel is hindered. R. C. Sproul speaks of a professor's attacks on Scripture during his college days:

> What stands out in my memory of those days is the heavy emphasis on biblical texts regarding the return of Christ, which were constantly cited as examples of errors in the New Testament and proof that the text had been edited to accommodate the crisis in the early church caused by the so-called parousia-delay of Jesus. In a word, much of the criticism leveled against the trustworthiness of Scripture was linked to questions regarding biblical eschatology. . . . Due to the crisis in confidence in the truth and authority of Scripture and the subsequent crisis regarding the real historical Jesus, eschatology must come to grips with the tensions of time-frame references in the New Testament.[96]

Preterists, then, consider more to be at stake in the Olivet Discourse than an in-house eschatological debate with futurists. If the time texts call for a first-century fulfillment that did not occur, Christianity is seriously hobbled before its foes. Preterists believe they rescue apologetics from this danger because their eschatology accepts the "plain" meaning of the time texts and shows how they were fulfilled. To the preterist, the futurist position evades the plain meaning of the texts and thus comprises an effective defense of the faith.

How shall these concerns be addressed? I certainly agree that the failed date-settings of popular futurist writers are an embarrassment to the cause of Christ. Biblical futurists need to speak out forcefully against date-setting, knowing that it is contrary to Christ's admonitions that no one can know the date of His return.

However, futurism cannot be abandoned simply because

---

96 Sproul, *The Last Days*, 14-15, 26.

some of its proponents have abused it.[97] Eschatology cannot be driven by perceived apologetic advantage. It must be driven by accurate biblical exegesis—something that preterism is sorely lacking.

Ultimately, the attacks of liberal critics will concern evidentialist apologists like Sproul more than the presuppositional apologist. The church does not need a new eschatological system simply because unbelievers question the return of Christ. The humble child of God should meet such skeptics with 2 Peter 3:3-7, which promises judgment against those mockers who say, "Where is the promise of His coming? For ever since the fathers fell asleep, all continues just as it was from the beginning of creation."

The student who notes these twin preterist concerns—the failure of past futurist writers and the attacks of liberal critics—will be able to account for them as he interacts with preterist writings. He will also be positioned to address the concerns of believers who have come under the influence of preterist teaching.

In that regard, Christian pastors should take seriously the appeal of preterism to the average man in the pew. By portraying the past sensationalism of some futurist writers, the preterist is able to cast all futurists in a negative light. That opens the door for him to introduce a seemingly more sane approach to biblical prophecy. The preterist's affirmation of the inerrancy of Scripture gains him an even more sympathetic hearing with the earnest, but unprepared, believer. The plausibility of preterism is then heightened even further when it quotes ancient historians that are new to the reader. In contrast to the sensationalistic futurists, the preterist appears as a sober student of Scripture who has done his homework. It would be a mistake to underestimate the appeal and effectiveness of that approach.

---

97 Otherwise, partial preterists would have to abandon their cause immediately in the face of the heretical teaching of hyper-preterism.

Preterism and the Future of Israel

Preterism dispenses with Israel as a nation and many prophetic passages that would otherwise prove embarrassing.

Consequently, the student who addresses preterism in-depth must be prepared to deal with the broader issues that will almost certainly come along with it. The future of Israel, and her distinction from the church, will be quickly invoked as the preterist asserts a final judgment against Israel in the first century. The student should be prepared to address these more fundamental issues when he encounters preterism.[98]

Those theological themes lead naturally into another preterist weakness. The perspective of the disciples who heard the Olivet Discourse had been shaped by the Old Testament promises to the nation of Israel. If Jesus was predicting the imminent destruction of Jerusalem and the end of the nation of Israel with "indisputable clarity," He can only be regarded as a colossal failure, because the disciples were still expecting the national restoration of Israel at the time of the ascension. Their words, "Lord, is it at this time You are restoring the kingdom to Israel?" (Acts 1:6) indicate that the Olivet Discourse had not crushed their hopes of national restoration. They were still expecting a future kingdom for ethnic Israel.[99] That is inconceivable from the preterist perspective.

98 For the distinction between Israel and the Church, see Robert Saucy, *The Church in God's Program*, (Chicago: Moody Press, 1972), 69-82.

99 John A. McLean, "Did Jesus Correct the Disciples' View of the Kingdon?" *Bibliotheca Sacra* 151 (April-June 1994), 227. In other words, if Jesus taught that Israel would be judged into extinction within the generation of the disciples, they completely missed the point. They did not expect an imminent destruction of the nation, they expected an imminent restoration of it. It is impossible to reconcile that expectation with Jesus' introductory admonition in the Olivet Discourse that the disciples guard themselves against being misled about the future (Matthew 24:4).

Preterism and Millennial Views

Some of the most vocal proponents of preterism are theonomic postmillennialists. They desperately need preterism. Postmillennialism ultimately requires increasing righteousness to usher in the return of Christ. A future tribulation is not consistent with those expectations. Postmillennialists benefit from the preterist viewpoint, because it puts the tribulation in the past and leaves it there.

Similarly, amillennialists benefit from the preterist's judgment on Israel (which would open the door for the transfer of Israel's blessings to the church), and the relegation to the past of prophetic events.

The more a millennial view highlights and depends on preterism, the more suspect the entire scheme is. Preterism is fatally and irretrievably flawed for several independent reasons.

Conclusion

Despite the superficially alluring features of preterism, it is clearly in error. The patient student of Scripture will find himself more than prepared to refute the doctrine of those who contradict. When one sifts through preterist teaching, he finds that history does not support preterism. Sound hermeneutics do not support preterism. Sound exegesis does not support preterism. On the testimony of two or three witnesses, a matter is established.

It is the better part of wisdom not to expect preterism to go away. Its proponents are sometimes clever writers who make a persuasive case. But preterism is not true. It will fail in the end.

In the meantime, Robert Thomas has set forth the response to preterism that will prove most effective over the long haul:

> Meeting its challenge will call for patient exegesis of the
> separate texts, the kind that requires much time. Yet it is

vital to spend this time in the text if the truth of the Word of God is to prevail over propagated error. May this be a call to all to handle the Scriptures carefully in the face of this and many other threats that tend to disfigure the face of Christian doctrine here at the end of the twentieth century. Though human efforts are feeble, may God help His servants to do a good job in what He has put them here to do.[100]

100 Thomas, "Theonomy and the Dating of Revelation," 202.

Appendix A: What About Israel Today?

Thus says the L<small>ORD</small>, "If My covenant for day and night stand not, and the fixed patterns of heaven and earth I have not established, then I would reject the descendants of Jacob and David My servant, not taking from his descendants rulers over the descendants of Abraham, Isaac and Jacob. But I will restore their fortunes and will have mercy on them."
(Jeremiah 33:25-26)

I say then, God has not rejected His people, has He? May it never be! For I too am an Israelite, a descendant of Abraham, of the tribe of Benjamin.
(Romans 11:1)

Appendix A is taken from an interview I did at Truth Community Church on October 31, 2023. The nation of Israel was at war with Hamas in the Gaza Strip. I was asked to give some biblical perspectives on Israel.

To discuss Israel in a biblical way would require multiple messages. So what I say here is brief and oversimplified, but hopefully it is enough to give us a framework for right thinking. I want to balance this around three different points.

The Current Military Situation

The modern nation of Israel has an absolute right and responsibility to protect itself from those who would destroy it. Genesis 9:6 says that if man sheds blood, by man his blood shall be shed, and in Romans 13, Scripture says government bears the sword in order to bring judgment on those who do evil. It is lawful for the Israeli government to wage this war against Hamas. After all, even God sent His people to war in the Old Testament. Israel has every right to do this to protect its citizens and bring retribution on those who made an unprovoked attack on civilians. I stand with Israel and its unfettered right to self-defense.

Yes, war is grievous. Innocent people suffer and die. If you go back to my message on Psalm 137 ("By the Rivers of Babylon") I go through some of the biblical history of war involving pagan nations. It is graphic. Scripture describes the wombs of pregnant women being ripped open and babies' heads being dashed. War is ugly and innocent people often suffer and die. That comes with the territory of war.

But when wicked people attack a sovereign nation, they must be neutralized so they cannot do further harm in the future. Israel is completely within their bounds to do whatever they think is necessary to protect their citizens. That would be true of any nation.

The stated policy of Hamas is the destruction of Israel. So what are the Jews supposed to do when Hamas attacks them? We need to see the current military situation as something in which they are exercising a national right to self-defense, which is perfectly appropriate and biblically justifiable.

The Current Spiritual Situation

But let's pivot from the current military situation to the current spiritual situation in Israel. No matter what you say about Israel spiritually, you invite criticism from all kinds of different theological perspectives.

We should not confuse Israel's human right of self-defense with their biblical position before God as they stand as a nation. Right now, the nation of Israel is under the judgment of God because they have rejected Christ as their Messiah.

Jesus mourned over Jerusalem in Luke 13:34-35 and 19:41-44. He would have gathered them under His wings but they would not have it. They rejected Christ and crucified Him with the help of the Romans. Collectively, they reject Christ to this day. As a result, they are not under the protection but rather the judgment of God. They are an unbelieving people. It's a grievous situation.

Paul speaks in Romans about how he's grieved for his kinsmen who are his according to the flesh. He acknowledges their zeal, but says it is not according to knowledge (cf. Rom. 9:1-5, 10:1-4). Nothing has changed since then.

We should not look at modern Israel as being the inheritors of the promises of God. (I will clarify that with my third point in just a moment.) As long as the Jews as a people continue to reject Jesus Christ as their Messiah, they will continue to experience chastisement and difficulty.

In Deuteronomy 28, you see the many curses that God lays upon the Jews when they reject Him. We need to keep that in mind. We should not confuse the nature of the biblical nation of Israel with the nature of the unbelieving nation today.

In the current military situation, it is righteous before God for them to pursue war. That is distinct from their current spiritual situation in which they're under judgment because they've rejected their own Messiah.

At the same time, we should remember that God has a remnant of believing Jews. I have friends in ministry who are converted Jews. Those individual believing Jews show that God has not abandoned the Jews completely.

But as a nation? There's a reason for their suffering.

The Future Restoration of Israel

As I understand Scripture, we should not confuse the current state of judgment as being an absolute and final judgment from God for all time. Many Christians hold that position. They say there's nothing left for Israel. God has supposedly transferred all the promises to the church.

I don't believe that that's the biblical case. God promised in Zechariah 12:10 that there would be a future time where He would pour out His Holy Spirit upon the Jews in the last day. As a result, the nation will look on Christ whom they had pierced with a spirit of repentance. That day is still future to us.

There is a coming day in which a future generation of the Jews will receive their Messiah. They will repent. When that happens, Christ will take the throne of David on earth and reign over the nations in a time of peace and prosperity that is known as the millennium. At that time, God will show that He has kept His promises to His people.

God made promises to Abraham. He made promises to David that there would be a throne upon which His Son would sit, reigning from Jerusalem. He made promises in the New Covenant in Jeremiah 31 that He would give Israel new life and a new heart to respond to Him. God would write His law on their hearts. And that's all still future.

Many Bible teachers say those promises have been taken

from Israel and transferred to the church so that they are fulfilled in the church in a spiritual way. I respect some of the
men who teach that, but that's not what I believe Scripture
teaches.

God made promises to Israel in the Old Testament that they
would have a land, their own king, and that they would experience the spiritual blessings of new life and forgiveness. The
physical land and physical ancestry are important aspects of
those promises. God's word to them must be fulfilled.

If you say that Israel forfeited all of that, and now it's being
fulfilled in the church in a spiritual way with spiritual blessings, you have stretched the word "fulfillment" beyond recog-
nition. Under that view, God's promise is not being fulfilled
on the physical terms in which it was originally given. It's not
being fulfilled to the physical people to whom the promise was
originally given. So by what contortion of human language can
we call that a "fulfillment"?

I see the language of Genesis 12, 2 Samuel 7, Jeremiah 31,
and other like texts and believe that future fulfillment, not
transfer, best satisfies what God promises. To say that the
church has replaced Israel renders so much Scripture inco-
herent.

Men reach that conclusion through an interpretational
approach that says you can reinterpret the Old Testament in
light of the New Testament. I don't agree with that approach. I
believe you take the Old Testament on its terms and interpret
the New Testament in a way that advances the Old Testament,
but does not change or reinterpret it. That is a big issue in biblical interpretation.

I would point you to Ezekiel 37:15-28 and further mention
that almost every one of the minor prophets speaks of a future
restoration of national Israel. I think those who deny a future
to national Israel neglect the minor prophets. The theme is too
prominent to miss. Now obviously, that spiritual restoration
of Israel has not happened since the first coming of Christ. It's
still future to us.

Understand that more than national Israel is at stake in this discussion. If we say that God cancelled the promises to Israel because of their apostasy at the time of Christ, we jeopardize everything we teach as Bible-believing Christians. God chose Israel. If He would reverse His promises to them because of their sin, what's to keep Him from reversing our election in Christ for our sin? Are we better than they?

So the character of God, the fidelity of God to His covenants and promises, are all wrapped up in our view of these things. Romans 9–11 bears on this as well. So while men I respect disagree on this issue, I think Scripture is clear. That is what we hold to. That is what we teach.

In summary, God promises that He will one day pour out His Spirit on Israel, give them a new heart, and they will repent over having crucified their Messiah. When that day comes, they will recite the things stated in Isaiah 53 as an expression of their repentance. Then, not only will God have gathered in Gentiles like us, He will gather in the Jews. God will be greatly glorified for His grace on the Gentiles and His grace on the Jews. Moreover, there will be a time of great peace and prosperity as Christ reigns over the earth.

Appendix B: What About Dispensationalism?

But as for you, speak the things which are fitting for sound doctrine.
(Titus 2:1)

In the same interview about modern Israel, I was asked about the term "dispensationalism." The edited transcript of my answer now follows.

Those of you who are informed on theological issues will recognize that what I just said about a future for national Israel and a reign of Christ on earth during the millennium has themes from what has traditionally been called a "dispensational" perspective. I acknowledge that. But I do not apply the term "dispensationalist" to myself. I think it confuses things rather than bringing clarity.

John MacArthur has defined dispensationalism as follows:

> Dispensationalism is a system of biblical interpretation that sees a distinction between God's program for Israel and His dealings with the church.[101]

If we use the term dispensational *strictly and only* to distinguish between Israel and the church and to indicate that the church has not replaced Israel in God's program, I can live with that. My prior answer about modern Israel explains my position on that basis.

The problem with dispensationalism *as a theological movement* over the past one hundred years is that it has brought so much false and destructive teaching that I cannot possibly use that term to describe myself. I oppose too much of the movement to use the label. Let me give you just a few examples.

101 John MacArthur, *The Gospel According to the Apostles* (Nashville: Word Publishing, 2000), 219. He devotes pages 219-233 to an analysis of dispensationalism which is worthy of close attention.

Dispensationalists have been known to say that the Sermon on the Mount is only for the future millennium. They have made a sharp distinction between the kingdom of God and the kingdom of heaven. Some dispensationalists have created the impression that they were saying there were two ways of salvation: law in the Old Testament; grace in the New Testament. Further, and without defining these terms, there are classic dispensationalists and progressive dispensationalists.

Who can make sense of all that?

Others teach that the moral law as expressed in the Ten Commandments is not binding as a rule of life for Christians. More recently, dispensationalists like Charles Ryrie and Zane Hodges have taught that you can receive Christ as Savior without receiving Him as Lord, and that repentance from sin is not necessary for salvation. Some call it "no-lordship salvation."

The root problem in that no-lordship teaching is an utter lack of understanding and explanation of the doctrine of regeneration. When God saves someone, He makes him *new* (cf. 2 Cor. 5:17). The new birth imparts a new heart that is given so that spiritual life and obedience to God inevitably flow forth (cf. 1 John 2:3-4). If you reduce conversion to simply saying a prayer to "ask Jesus into your heart," and ignore regeneration, you put souls in danger. False conversion is a dangerous and common phenomenon, as Jesus made clear in Matthew 7:21-23.

That no-lordship teaching, which is the fruit of modern dispensationalism, makes a mess of so many things. It seals unsuspecting people in self-deception. It puts their souls in eternal danger. In the meantime, it undermines accountability and church discipline in the life of a local church. We cannot tolerate any of that in ministry.

The term "dispensationalism," then, has so much baggage that you need a mile-long freight train to transport it all. No wonder Pastor MacArthur went on to say:

> Frankly, some mongrel species of dispensationalism ought to die, and I will be happy to join the cortege.[102]

That's why I don't apply the term to myself. It can only create confusion rather than advancing my goal in ministry, which is to teach the Bible with clarity so that the saints will grow in grace and unbelievers will be converted to Christ.

I prefer the term "futuristic premillennialist." That is specific. It limits the consideration to eschatology. *Futuristic* indicates that we believe the tribulation is still future (not past as preterists claim) and that there is a future for national Israel. *Pre*millennial says that Christ will return before the millennium happens. Pre*millennial* says we believe in a 1000-year reign of Christ on the earth.

Many will still disagree with that position, but at least we have narrowed it to the points at hand. If a term creates hopeless confusion, you need something that better describes your position. That's why I avoid "dispensationalism" as a term to describe my theological convictions.

I have friends who will probably be disappointed with what I just said. But the ones who are committed to charity and clarity will at least understand why I do not use the term, even if they are content to use it themselves. I'll use "futuristic premillennialist" and fair-minded people who understand eschatology will know what I'm saying.

---

102 Ibid., 221.

Appendix C: What About the Baptist Confession of 1689?

Pay close attention to yourself and to your teaching; persevere in these things, for as you do this you will ensure salvation both for yourself and for those who hear you.
(1 Timothy 4:16)

Pastors and theological students sometimes ask me about the relationship between futuristic premillennialism and The Baptist Confession of Faith of 1689. It is a fair question. Truth Community Church uses the 1689 as our confession of faith. (That confession is readily available online.)

Chapters 31-32 in the 1689 cover matters of eschatology in a briefer, more general way than what I have set forth in this book. Many who hold to the 1689 would disagree with what I have written, and some accordingly would question whether it is consistent for our church to hold to the 1689. I offer this brief explanation.

I believe the 1689 gives room for futuristic premillennialism because it does not deny the doctrines I have presented here. The 1689: (1) does not equate Israel with the Church; (2) does not assert that the Church has replaced Israel; (3) does not deny a future for national Israel; and (4) does not explicitly deny a future millennium during which Christ will reign on the earth. For those reasons, I do not believe it contradicts the system of doctrine in the 1689 to affirm, as secondary, matters on which the Confession itself is silent.

In that regard, I think it is significant that a scholarly exposition of 1689, which explicitly rejects premillennial theology, nevertheless concedes that "the Confession says nothing specific about premillennialism" and "It may be true that the authors of the Confession did not wish to denounce explicitly a doctrine held by some whom they may have regarded as brethren."[103]

Others agree with that assessment. One commentator on the 1689, after reviewing support for amillennialism, post-millennialism, and "chiliasm" (another term for premillennialism) says: "Any of these opinions may have been held by and accepted among confessional Baptists. . . . There was room, even within a close confessional theology, for differences of outlook."[104]

Still another recent writer on the 1689 says:

> Over the centuries, eschatology has become a hotly debated issue, sometimes leading to bitter divisions among professing Christians. We must note that the Baptists saw no reason to disagree with anything the Presbyterians and Congregationalists had to say about these subjects in their Confessions.[105]

Even Charles Spurgeon, a strong proponent of the 1689 Confession, is quoted as saying:

> I think that the millennium will commence after his coming, and not before it. I cannot imagine the Kingdom with the King absent.[106]

For all these reasons, I am satisfied that one can hold to the system of doctrine taught in the 1689 Confession and teach futuristic premillennialism.

---

103 Sam Waldron, *A Modern Exposition of the 1689 Baptist Confession of Faith* (Darlington, Co. Durham, England: Evangelical Press, 1989), 416.

104 James M. Renihan, *To the Judicious and Impartial Reader: An Exposition of the 1689 London Baptist Confession of Faith* (Cape Coral, Florida: Founders Press, 2022), 573.

105 Jim Doom, in Rob Ventura, gen. ed., *A New Exposition of the Longdon Baptist Confession of Faith of 1689* (Scotland: Mentor, 2022), 522.

106 Charles Spurgeon, *Exploring the Heart and Mind of the Prince of Preachers,* ed. Kerry James Allen (Oswego, IL: Fox River Press, 2005),144.

THE TRUTH PULPIT

Teaching God's People God's Word

To learn more about Don Green and his Bible-teaching resources, visit thetruthpulpit.com. You can subscribe to podcasts of his full-length messages from Truth Community Church, the daily "The Truth Pulpit" audio program, and his weekly feature "Through the Psalms."

Also by Don Green

The Bible tells us to expect difficult trials as part of the Christian life. You know that you should trust God when hard times come, but exactly how do you trust God when life seems to fall apart at the seams? This life-changing study from the book of Habakkuk will teach you how to move from trials to spiritual triumph—even if your circumstances do not change.

> "No matter who you are or where you are in life, I know you will benefit greatly from Pastor Green's insights on the prophecy of Habakkuk and the problem of human misery."
> — John MacArthur: from *The Foreword*

> ". . . blessings overflow in encouragement and comfort for all who will read it and take its counsel to heart."
> —Tom Ascol: Pastor, Grace Baptist Church of Cape Coral, FL; President of Founders Ministries and The Institute of Public Theology

Trusting God in Trying Times: Studies in the Book of Habakkuk
Hardcover, 128pp
ISBN 978-0-9987156-1-2
www.ttwpress.com

Also by Don Green

Scripture calls believers to "examine everything carefully" (1 Thessalonians 5:21) and to "test the spirits to see whether they are from God" (1 John 4:1). In this book, Don Green defends the four Gospels from scholarly theories that would undermine confidence in the words of Christ recorded in God's inspired Word. Academic yet accessible, this book will help you develop lifelong principles of discernment and strengthen your view of the authority of Scripture—the sacred text which is essential for true faith and eternal life.

Did Jesus REALLY Say?
Examining a Scholarly Threat to the Gospels
Hardcover, 122pp
ISBN 978-0-9987156-2-9
www.ttwpress.com

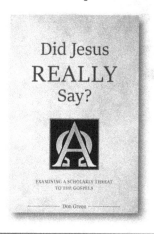

Also by Don Green
•••••••••••••••••••••••••••

John MacArthur began his ministry at Grace Community Church in Sun Valley, California in 1969. Since then, millions have known him as a steadfast voice for biblical authority and teaching. But what kind of man is he in private? Don Green observed him closely over a fifteen-year period in leadership roles at Grace Church and Grace to You. *In John MacArthur: An Insider's Tribute*, you'll find winsome vignettes, exclusive interviews, and never-before-published photos to give you access to the man whose service to Christ has benefitted so many—all as a testimony to the grace of God in the life of John MacArthur.

John MacArthur: An Insider's Tribute
Deluxe Coffee-Table Quality Hardback, Color Throughout, 80pp
ISBN 978-0-9987156-0-5
www.ttwpress.com

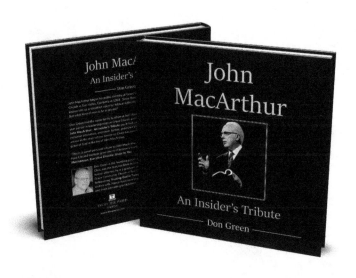

Printed in the USA
CPSIA information can be obtained
at www.ICGtesting.com
LVHW022359280124
769654LV00001B/1